Robert of Arbrissel

JACQUES DALARUN

Robert of Arbrissel

SEX, SIN, AND SALVATION IN
THE MIDDLE AGES

Translated with an
introduction and notes by

BRUCE L. VENARDE

With a new preface by the author

The Catholic University of America Press
Washington, D.C.

Ouvrage publié avec le concours du Ministère français chargé
de la culture—
Centre national du livre.
This work has been published with the support of the French Ministry
of Culture, National Center for the Book.

LIBRARY OF CONGRESS CATALOGING-IN-PUBLICATION DATA

Dalarun, Jacques.

[Robert d'Arbrissel fondateur de Fontevraud. English]

Robert of Arbrissel: sex, sin, and salvation in the Middle Ages / Jacques
Dalarun ; translated with an introduction and notes by Bruce L. Venarde ;
with a new preface by the author.— 1st ed.

p. cm.

Includes bibliographical references and index.

ISBN-13: 978-0-8132-1439-9 (pbk. : alk. paper)

ISBN-10: 0-8132-1439-4 (pbk. : alk. paper)

1. Robert, of Arbrissel, ca. 1045–1117.   2. Monastic and religious life—
France—History—Middle Ages, 600–1500.   3. Catholic Church—
France—Clergy—History.   4. Abbaye de Fontevrault—History.
I. Venarde, Bruce L., 1962–   II. Title.

BX4705.R567D35 2006

271'.79—dc22

2005014045

CONTENTS

TWENTY YEARS AFTER

A New Preface by Jacques Dalarun

This book is young—twenty years old. Published in France in 1986, it presented the results of my first research project in medieval history, an investigation of the dossier on Robert of Arbrissel conducted for a doctoral thesis.

From the beginning, I had been struck by a paradox. Medieval European society held out as models certain individuals, the saints, who in fact never missed an opportunity to challenge the established order. Nowadays people tend to identify with archetypes of social success, the rich, powerful, and famous. In the past, however, the admired were men and women who deliberately turned their backs on worldly values. Sainthood thus reveals a more general phenomenon, the Christian paradox of medieval society: Christianity pervaded the entire Middle Ages in the West, but its Gospel is particularly badly suited to serve as the dominant ideology of a social order. The saints are only one indication of this enduring discrepancy.

To measure this divergence between sanctity and the establishment, my thesis director, Pierre Toubert, pointed me to materials concerning the hermits of western France at the turn of the twelfth century, an era profoundly marked by what is usually called "the Gregorian Reform," a movement of ecclesiastical reorganization and moral purification named after its exponent Pope Gregory VII. Most of this group of holy people had experienced phases of the hermit's retreat, itinerant preaching, and finally ended their journeys as founders of religious communities. I began to read the printed *vitae*, the saints' Lives, of William Firmatus, Bernard of Tiron, Vitalis of Savigny, and Robert of Arbrissel. Then Pierre Toubert encouraged me to consult manuscript sources. This was a revelation: the historian's work was not only to say in other words what was already known, but could also consist in presenting forgotten testimonies about the past to promote knowledge and understanding.

Through a combination of determination and fate, I had the good fortune to discover, in a Middle French manuscript housed at the Bibliothèque Nationale in Paris, a version of the second Life of Robert of Arbrissel far longer than the surviving Latin text. Robert was the most daring of my four holy musketeers. Not content with preaching the renunciation of the world and leading crowds in the wooded solitudes of western France, he founded at Fontevraud a monastery of men and women where the former were under the authority of the latter. The unpublished end of the second Life revealed in particular the instructions Robert gave to both sexes right up to his death on February 25, 1116. The Middle French text furthermore narrated in detail the quarrels that broke out over who would hold onto Robert's mortal remains, which were finally laid to rest at the right side of the high altar in the abbey church of Font-evraud on March 7, 1116.

This discovery changed my research plans. My doctoral thesis, defended in 1984 and published the next year under the title *L'impossible sainteté: La Vie retrouvée de Robert d'Arbrissel (v. 1045–1116), fondateur de Fontevraud*, revolved around this important unpublished material from the Bibliothèque Nationale: identification, authentication, study of its circulation and use, hypotheses about the reasons for its partial eclipse, edition, and commentary. In the end, it sufficed to let this unknown text speak for itself, for the face of Robert of Arbrissel, the plan that underlay his strange foundation, and the responses he aroused among his contemporaries all necessarily emerged in a new light.

Georges Duby, who had in 1984 just published *William Marshall*, urged me, my thesis barely defended, to write a biography of Robert of Arbrissel. That meant a radical change of perspective. *L'impossible sainteté* was the story of a text. Now I had to produce the story of an individual. The genre of biography posed two questions of principle. First, in focusing attention on an individual destiny, I feared turning aside from the broader collective movements that should be the heart of historians' preoccupations. Was writing a biography yielding to the shallow pleasure of storytelling? Secondly, I doubted my ability to get at the truth about an individual. To meld testimonies about Robert that portrayed him at the same time so favorably and so unfavorably—would such a process not obscure whatever made him unique?

I dismissed the first concern easily. Robert of Arbrissel was known principally through two Lives, two texts that belong to the genre of narrative in general and that of hagiography in particular. His hagiographers, the narrators of his holiness, wrote because they were convinced of their hero's exemplary nature. Even if he retires to the desert, a saint is never utterly alone. His holiness is based on a relationship, perhaps to God, certainly to his contemporaries. The individual becomes a model for the society from which he came. To produce a biography with proper historical value, it sufficed to trace the threads of hagiographic accounts, always interweaving moral and religious exemplarity and its distinctive social and cultural context.

The second reservation, though, seemed more serious. However, the dilemma was not new and the solution had already been masterfully proposed by Arsenio Frugoni in his *Arnaldo da Brescia nelle fonti del secolo XII*: do not blend the sources together, but listen to each of them for what it says until the historic person, far from flattened into dullness through the method of simple combination, emerges vividly in the contrasting light of different testimonies. I took the same lessons from a novel by Vladimir Nabokov, *The Real*

Life of Sebastian Knight. This book tells the story of a man who learns of the death of a half-brother he had rarely seen. He questions those who knew his half-brother, both intimately and casually, and gets irreconcilable profiles from all concerned. If there is a truth about Sebastian Knight, it lies at the intersection of these contradictory memories. To this day, I think of the historian's craft this way: it is our attempt to approach the truth about a dead man who might almost have been our half-brother.

A careful reading of the book that follows will show it carries the traces of these preliminary reflections. To ensure there is a connection between the history of a man and the history of his time, the whole work is driven by constant movement between the general and the particular, the individual and the collective. As regards Robert of Arbrissel, though, each chapter only echoes a selection of the sources that contribute to an understanding of him. After an introductory chapter that presents the places Robert traversed, from Arbrissel to Fontevraud, and the texts that preserve his memory, Chapter Two mainly follows the first Life by Baudri of Bourgueil. Chapter Three is based on two critical letters that Bishop Marbode of Rennes and Abbot Geoffrey of Vendôme addressed to the itinerant-preacher-become-founder. The fourth chapter, divided into four parts, relies on fragmentary sources like those of the miracle of the brothel of Rouen, Robert's letter to Countess Ermengarde of Brittany, and the miracle of Menat. Finally, Chapters Five and Six take their inspiration from the second Life attributed to the chaplain Andreas. The last word is his.

When this book was translated into German in 1987, into Italian in 1989, and into Portuguese in 1990, it was in the wake of its French publication of 1986. Its English translation, on the other hand, causes me to reread it at twenty years' distance. If I were to rewrite it, this would probably not be any longer the same book. Nevertheless, in agreement with the director of the Catholic University of America Press, David J. McGonagle, and the translator,

Bruce L. Venarde, I rejected the idea of an updated version. There would have been something artificial in such repair work. As Bruce Venarde usefully shows in his introduction, notes, and an invaluable bibliography, the study of Robert of Arbrissel, particularly in English, has gone forward in these last two decades, sometimes in response to my own research. Any attempt to reconcile all these points of view would have been a concession to the combination method and therefore inconsistent with the very intention of the original book. The enlightening introduction to this English edition situates my work of 1986 in historiographical perspective and presents the book for exactly what it is: not the definitive truth about Robert of Arbrissel, but a moment of historical research. To what extent have these subsequent publications confirmed, challenged, or redirected my perspective?

My work in 1986 was based solely on written sources. It is now impossible to consider Fontevraud without attention to the remarkable archeological investigations accomplished since then under the direction of Daniel Prigent. These excavations have rewritten the history of Fontevraud's foundation. As regards the founder, archeology has made two exciting discoveries. On the right-hand side of the high altar of the abbey church, the stone tomb in which Robert's body was laid to rest on March 7, 1116, has been restored. However, on the outside of the church, at its east end to be exact, archeologists found hollowed-out tombs in the earth where nuns and brothers lay in final repose. Written sources and archeological excavations thus act in perfect harmony to reveal the place where Robert was buried—and also the place where, as the account of his chaplain Andreas tells us, he had so very much wanted to be buried.

If there is a field in which historical research has progressed impressively in the last twenty years, it is that of medieval religious institutions. Historians have recognized that they have tended to project into all monastic history a very centralized model of order that did not truly emerge before the thirteenth century under the

influence of the mendicants, above all the Franciscans and Domini-
cans. Before that a different logic applied, one of houses and networks, a practice of federation that preceded the ideal of centralization. Against this backdrop, the originality and modernity of
Fontevraud are all the more striking. Penny Schine Gold underlined that Robert of Arbrissel's foundation experienced very precocious institutionalization. The oldest statutes of Fontevraud, which
I was lucky enough to discover recently, only confirm this conclusion. From the beginning, Robert conceived of his foundation as a
prototype of centralization, with a single abbess having full authority over the motherhouse and dependent establishments that thereby could have only the status of priories.

There could be an infinite number of discussions as to the significance of the relations between men and women in Fontevraud's
religious community. But complexity should not mask a reality
that seems all the clearer to me today: in setting up a body of religious men, clerics, and lay converts, all pledged to serve the nuns
and totally under the authority of the abbess, Robert resolved in
one action and for the next seven centuries the problem of the *cura
monialium*, the sacerdotal care of nuns. The matter would tear other communities apart, for we know that in most religious movements with both masculine and feminine branches, the men grum-
bled about having to concern themselves with the women, thinking
that they had more noble things to accomplish than dedicating
themselves to the service of nuns. At Fontevraud, Robert solved
the problem before it ever arose.

Next come the more personal aspects of Robert's story. Did I
place too much importance on the hypothesis that his father was a
cleric, the parish priest of Arbrissel? Did I show too much imagination in supposing that Robert, too, had known the pleasures of the
flesh, as the authors of the time said? I have recently discovered an
unexpurgated Latin copy of Baudri's Life of Robert, one not shorn

of its most burning passages. Here is exactly what the text says on the subject:

> The blessed Robert of whom we have resolved to speak was indeed a son and heir of the Christian profession and a scion of lower Brittany, which province he adorned as a priest and the progeny of priests. He was born in the territory of Rennes, a native inhabitant of the village called Arbrissel. And his father was named Damalioch, his mother Orguende. In short, it is reported that this Robert, the son of a priest, from boyhood strove to expiate his father's vice and his own, if there was any, and from boyhood too began to develop the habits of maturity. (*Fuit igitur beatus de quo loqui disposuimus Robertus, christianae professionis co-haeres et filius, Britanniae minoris alumnus, quam provinciam decoravit sacerdos ex sacerdotibus progenitus, ex pago Redonensi oriundus, villae quae vulgo Arbriscellum nuncupatur indigena et colonus. Pater autem ipsius Damaliochus, mater vero Orguendis nominabatur. Ipse denique Robertus, ut dictum est, presbyteri filius, a puero patris suumque, si quod erat, vitium piare studuit, et ab ipsa pueritia maturis moribus inolescere coepit.*)

Considering the perfect catalogue of virtues that a saint's Life is supposed to be, we must admit that the shocking mention of Robert's "vice" surely means something a little more than impure thoughts.

Still, should there be such stress on the importance of Robert's sense of guilt? Did I make an anachronistic Dostoyevskian hero out of the parish priest of Arbrissel, or give too much weight to personal anecdote? In the passage just quoted and which, it bears emphasizing, opens Baudri's account of Robert's terrestrial life, the hagiographer himself places his hero's entire life in the shadow of expiation. Most of all, consciousness of sin and feelings of guilt are more than a personal detail concerning Robert. They were, rather, among the most powerful weapons of the Gregorian movement, tools for constructing a new Christian Church from a model the reformers created. Let us, for a moment, put Robert's torments of conscience in the perspective of a broader history.

The Gregorian Reform bears as its stamp the name of Gregory VII, pope from 1073 to 1085. For the papacy, this movement of renewal was above all a struggle for political emancipation, meant to dismantle imperial patronage and disengage monks and priests from the feudal networks in which they naturally took part. Rejection of lay intervention in the election to ecclesiastical office; barring hereditary transmission of these offices that had become properties; the eradication of simony (trade in offices); and nicolaism (priestly marriage) were preliminary structures for a reconquest of the ecclesiastical machinery. Since in the absence of papal legions political warfare could not be resolved in military combat, it moved onto moral terrain. It suited papal purposes to persuade every Christian that he was a sinner, to exacerbate in every individual the sense of guilt. The contemporaries of Robert of Arbrissel never ceased lamenting their sins.

The notion of conscience, of course, was not invented at this time. A reading of his *Confessions* shows that St. Augustine (354–430) was well equipped with it, but the new Gregorian ecclesiology changed its meaning. It was no longer the Church that came first, welcoming mingled masses of the faithful to its breast. Henceforth the sum of individual members, each a living stone, constituted the ecclesiastical edifice. This tremendous reversal was intended, for the time being, to gather the collectivity of consciences into an army impossible to defeat because it was impossible to seize. In time, the change conferred on belief—and hence on deviance and disbelief—a power capable of shaking the temple of which it was now the foundation. This new scheme began with individual sins. Robert's faults, his repentance, and his expiation were not only the marks of a tormented soul but also a sign of the times.

I hold to these aspects of the present book. However, in reading historians writing in English, in particular, I judge that I treated poorly one of the principal actors in this story: the abbess Petronilla of Chemillé, who in the autumn of 1115 succeeded Robert as the director of Fontevraud. In reading and rereading the cartulary of the abbey—its collection of documents of which the great historian of Fontevraud, Jean-Marc Bienvenu, prepared an edition recently published thanks to the work of Robert Favreau and Georges Pon —and in seeing in those documents Abbess Petronilla negotiating as an equal with the highest ecclesiastical officials and leading lay authorities, I have taken note that Robert of Arbrissel's foundation, by the preeminence of women in it, managed a real inversion of values and positions. In analyzing the different versions of the statutes of Fontevraud, I have better understood that Petronilla, in her way, showed a sincere faithfulness to Robert's vision during her long abbacy (1115–1149).

I continue to think that the second Life devoted to the founder of Fontevraud was the object of intentional cutting and I persist in believing that Petronilla of Chemillé was its instigator. Still, I willingly admit that I made too much of the differences between the chaplain Andreas, author of the second Life, and the abbess. In proposing that lopping off the end of the second Life had as its goal to mask a lack of fidelity to Robert's intentions, I surely attributed ill intent to Petronilla. I see much more clearly now that this mutilation of the end of Andreas's account was a desperate maneuver meant to safeguard the canonization of the founder of Fontevraud. On September 1, 1119, the statutes of Fontevraud were presented to Pope Calixtus II (1119–1124) during his visit to the abbey. I am convinced that the hagiographic dossier on Robert was also submitted to the pope on this occasion, in the hopes of obtaining canonization of the founder. The statutes were formally approved, but the Lives went unmentioned. After this failure, probably, Petronilla wanted to suppress whatever material from the account of Andreas that might have displeased the pope. The ploy, of course, did not work.

At twenty years' distance, the English translation of this biography of Robert of Arbrissel proves that the historical process never allows us to wait for a definitive truth and that all research is enriched by debates, even those it provokes. I offer to David J. McGonagle my deepest thanks for having wanted to publish this book of my youth under the prestigious auspices of the Catholic University of America Press.

I wish to express my profound gratitude to Bruce L. Venarde. An excellent translator, he is above all a first-class historian. His *Women's Monasticism and Medieval Society: Nunneries in France and England, 890–1215*, published in 1997, is the authoritative study of questions central to the history of Fontevraud. In 2003, he presented English-speaking readers with the complete dossier of sources concerning Robert of Arbrissel in a work published by the Catholic University of America Press. With his introduction, his notes, and his bibliography, he has markedly increased the value of the present volume. Under his elegant pen and in the spirit of dialogue between historians of two worlds, I hope that this twenty-year-old book will find a new youth on this side of the Atlantic.

Jacques Dalarun
St. Bonaventure University
March 2005

ROBERT OF ARBRISSEL AND
HIS HISTORIANS

An Introduction by Bruce L. Venarde

This book traces the strange odyssey of Robert of Arbrissel (ca. 1045–1116). Born in eastern Brittany, the son of the village priest, it is likely Robert succeeded his father in that post. As a young man eager for more advanced education than his local environment could offer and yielding to the wanderlust that would characterize the rest of his life, Robert left his native territory. He went east to Paris, where he studied for some years. He returned at the behest of Bishop Sylvester de La Guerche to his home diocese of Rennes in Brittany, where he served for several years in the post of archpriest, working to reform the education and morality of the clergy. When his patron bishop died, he departed Rennes, spending a few more years in study at the cathedral school in Angers. Hungering for deep religious experience, Robert left Angers to begin life as a hermit in the forest of Craon, not far from his native Arbrissel. He was not lonely for long, though, since his holy way of life and charisma attracted many disciples, who eventually formed a house of canons called La Roë. The formalizing of the community took place in the winter of 1096 and in the presence of Pope Urban II, who summoned Robert to Angers. Impressed with the hermit's eloquence, the pope gave Robert the charge of public preaching. A few years later Robert left La Roë for full-time evangelism.

As a preacher, too, Robert drew a crowd. In 1101, he settled his followers at Fontevraud, which quickly grew into a prosperous monastery and the head of a small federation of religious houses by the time its founder died fifteen years later. Robert did not stay to supervise this foundation, either, continuing to travel and preach until he died, crisscrossing France, from Normandy in the north to Gascony in the south, a homeless rambler. A few months before his death, Robert established Fontevraud as an abbey, a mixed community of women and men in religious life under the authority of an abbess. In fact, Fontevraud was already well on its way to becoming what it remained until the French Revolution: the largest and wealthiest order of monasteries for women in Europe. Robert was buried in its abbey church in late winter of 1116.

Robert of Arbrissel's idiosyncrasy and restlessness were alluring to many; he attracted many followers and patrons to his religious foundations, both great secular lords like the mighty counts of Anjou and ecclesiastical officials like Robert's friend Bishop Peter of Poitiers. Many of his devotees were women, of varied class and status, some said to be concubines or prostitutes. Perhaps for this reason most of all, Robert was a disturbing figure. The first accounts we have of Robert date to his lifetime, in the form of two letters from a bishop and an abbot, criticizing what their authors regarded as religious practices dangerous to both Robert and the enthusiasts his evident charisma inspired. Very shortly after his death, two men wrote biographical accounts, Latin *vitae* ("lives") that stressed Robert's holiness.

These four Latin documents—the letters from Bishop Marbode of Rennes and Abbot Geoffrey of Vendôme and the *vitae* by Baudri of Bourgueil, the archbishop of Dol, and Brother Andreas of Fontevraud—provide nearly all the contemporary information about Robert of Arbrissel. It is on them that Jacques Dalarun bases the account that follows. Adhering closely to the words of four people who knew Robert and had heard plenty more about him from others, the author provides an interpretive account of his life and works. It was a life that played out in a dynamic and creative period of European history, the time in which the foundations of Western society as we know it were laid. It was an age of economic growth, military and political ambition, and all sorts of ideas about the ordering of society, including early versions of everything from the separation of church and state to Christian marriage. This introduction will not further anticipate Dalarun's fascinating narrative, written in a vivid style of popular history familiar to French readers and replicated in large part in the present translation. It aims instead to put Dalarun's enterprise in the context of earlier commentary on Robert and the kinds of work historians of medieval France were doing when this book first appeared in 1986. It will then touch on other scholarship concerning Robert of Arbrissel that has appeared in the last thirty years, much of it in the wake of Dalarun's study. There are other perspectives on Robert of Arbrissel, other interpretations of his peculiarities, but Dalarun's vision of the man, expressed through its careful yet inventive presentation of the medieval sources, continues to carry weight two decades later.

JACQUES DALARUN'S ROBERT OF ARBRISSEL

As a graduate student, Jacques Dalarun made a surprising discovery while researching in the French National Library in Paris. During a quest for material related to the history of the abbey of Fontevraud, he examined a manuscript from about 1500 containing translations into French of the two Latin *vitae* of Robert of Arbrissel. The French version of the account by Andreas, though, turned out to be considerably longer than the Latin text. Comparing the Latin and French versions, Dalarun concluded that the longer version of the second *vita* was a faithful rendering of Andreas's original text, now lost, that expanded by approximately forty percent the length of this account. This material offered new details about Robert's final days and his death, the conflict over where his body was to be buried (including a kidnapping of his corpse), and the eventual return of Robert's mortal remains for burial at Fontevraud, the abbey he had founded fifteen years earlier. Analyzing the full version of Andreas's narrative in light of a thorough re-reading of all that had been written about Robert of Arbrissel since the Middle Ages, Dalarun formulated an original interpretation of his life first offered in his highly erudite 1985 work *L'impossible sainteté: La Vie retrouvée de Robert d'Arbrissel (v. 1045–1116), fondateur de Fontevraud* (with a preface by his university research director, Pierre Toubert), which was developed in the present, more accessible book a year later. Other than some additional information on a holy man's last hours and the days up to his burial, what, exactly, was new about Dalarun's Robert of Arbrissel?

For much of the early modern period (roughly 1500–1800), writers on Robert of Arbrissel wrote to judge him, either as a misunderstood saint or a sexual predator. Those who wrote in Robert's defense had to explain the close association with women that is a theme of his life and a subject of criticism in the letters of both Marbode of Rennes and Geoffrey of Vendôme. Particularly worrisome was Robert's practice, described by both medieval critics, of sleeping among women, apparently a penitential practice meant to mortify the flesh by tempting it exceedingly. Some advocates called these letters character assassination without basis in fact. One abbess of the seventeenth century, trying to have Robert recognized as a saint, went so far as to send deputies to Vendôme to remove the offending item from the original twelfth-century manuscript of Abbot Geoffrey's collected letters, literally to cut it out of the book. (Fortunately for posterity, it had been printed some years earlier.) Nevertheless, suspicions remained, and Robert's canonization was not effected at that time—or at any point since, for that matter. In the eighteenth century, the anticlerical polymath Voltaire inserted in his satirical poem on Joan of Arc a few sarcastic lines about the "great saint" Robert, who slept between two plump nuns, allowing him to caress four ample buttocks and breasts—without sinning.

More nuanced interpretations of Robert emerged after 1800. In the first chapter of this book, Dalarun refers briefly to two of the most important. The patriotic historian Jules Michelet wrote sympathetically of Robert's contribution to French civilization, in particular his sponsorship of women's religious enthusiasm through accepting their company and founding Fontevraud and its daughter houses, mixed communities of men and women where the latter were numerically superior and held all positions of authority. Since Michelet, historians working from his ideas have seen in Robert of Arbrissel an early advocate of the cult of courtly love, with its exaltation of women and the feminine, or even a precursor of modern feminism. A second line of interpretation is based not only on gender ideology but also and more importantly consideration of material conditions. This view of Robert's mission emphasized his criticism, to a socially diverse audience, of the medieval clergy and nobility for their wealth and immorality. Robert's desire for the liberation of the oppressed included the freeing of women from slavery to men, but, this interpretation argued, it was economic at its base, a protest against privilege and poverty.

Using the new material he had discovered, Dalarun pursued a fresh interpretive agenda. In order to take Robert of Arbrissel seriously as an impassioned Christian seeker, Dalarun devoted his considerable powers of learning to understanding Robert, insofar as possible, from the less than objective sources of critical letters and admiring *vitae*. This was, at the time, a rather unusual intellectual project for a young French scholar. The study of France in the central Middle Ages (1000–1300) was then primarily focused on social history and political history. Scholars investigated the complexities of worldly power, personal relations and social networks, judicial and juridical developments, and economic patterns and concerns (rural as well as urban and commercial, this latter emerging strongly out of an earlier, largely agricultural basis of wealth in the twelfth century). It is probably fair to say that this research agenda, shared by a whole generation of scholars, was little concerned with the specifically religious aspects of Christianity in the period: bishops were powerful lords and abbots great proprietors. Questions of spirituality and sanctity, both difficult and specialized historical subjects, were beside the main interests of most medieval historians in the 1960s, 1970s, and 1980s. In reaction to an outdated vision of the Middle Ages as a Catholic golden age, those who did study belief frequently argued that whatever was real about medieval religious practice was popular and what was popular was largely folkloric, semi-Christian at best.

Probably the greatest of the generation of French medievalists preceding Dalarun's was Georges Duby, whose interests in the first part of a long and prolific career tended toward the organization of medieval economy and social relations. Duby's interests in property, family, and lineage led him, in the 1970s and beyond, to the study of women, marriage, and gender in the eleventh and twelfth century, subjects clearly central to any consideration of Robert of Arbrissel, who drew such attention in his lifetime for surrounding himself with spiritual women, including unhappily married ones. Duby was pessimistic about the possibilities for uncovering the real lives of medieval women, so often reflected through the eyes of men; furthermore, at the time Dalarun was investigating Robert of Arbrissel and Fontevraud, Duby had written almost nothing about religious women. Dalarun wanted to investigate more deeply the history of women.

Dalarun, then, was taking up threads of other scholarly fabrics, but with a design very much his own. To take medieval religion, hagiography (texts concerning saints and sanctity), and gender seriously was not an obvious path to success in the French academic world of Dalarun's youth; it was a courageous approach to a career. Nonetheless, inspired by his own discovery of new matter on Robert of Arbrissel and encouraged by the appearance of two recent major works on medieval Christian spirituality (1975) and sanctity (1981) by André Vauchez, Dalarun pushed ahead with his examination of the medieval dossier of Robert of Arbrissel.

Dalarun chose to neither praise nor damn. Instead of presenting Robert as proto-feminist or proto-socialist, he tried to understand him in his own historical context as a devout Christian with a powerful spiritual agenda derived in large part from a profound sense of unworthiness and sinfulness, sexual and otherwise. He also, as will be clear to the readers of this book, examined surviving texts with great sensitivity to their purposes, their genres, and their limitations as well as to the opportunities they present for comprehending one perplexing man's career. In Dalarun's hands, Robert's story is about a man and his experience, about the trajectory of change in his time, in particular as regards the functions and meanings of Christianity with special attention to gender and sexuality. The book draws readers into the complex but rewarding task of uncovering all of that from documents that ask different questions and provide different answers than do modern readers. Robert emerges as a man of his age, very different from our own, but in Dalarun's hands a sympathetic figure, heroic not as class warrior or feminist but as uncompromising spiritual seeker.

ROBERT OF ARBRISSEL SINCE 1986

Dalarun's idiosyncratic choice of subject matter—perhaps not entirely unrelated to the alluring peculiarity of Robert himself—was quasi-prophetic. In the past twenty years, scholarship on all aspects of medieval Christianity has proliferated. Studies of popes and saints, monasticism, the place of women in Christian thought and practice, the relations of Christian institutions and secular power, and theology now abound. A few examples relevant to Robert of Arbrissel will suffice to make the point. Two men much

like Robert who figure in the present book, the wandering preachers Vitalis of Savigny and Bernard of Tiron, now have each been
carefully analyzed in scholarly studies. Gregory VII, the pope
whose program of reform had enormous influence on Robert's life,
was the subject in 1998 of a massive biography, the first in English
since the 1930s. The last decade has also seen much new work in
several languages on both the sources for Gregory's pontificate
and the classic themes of Church law and ecclesiastical politics in
Robert of Arbrissel's lifetime. The place of women in medieval
Christianity, as nuns, thinkers, artists, and patrons, is now revealed
in almost countless studies. All this investigation, furthermore, has
made it quite clear that there is much more to learn about all these
people and subjects.

In the 1980s, young Jacques Dalarun gambled that the intrin-
sic significance of his intellectual interests would become clear to
other scholars. He was right. The book translated here remains the
most recent full-length study of Robert of Arbrissel, but this curious figure has continued to elicit a variety of interpretations and
analyses, both closely resembling Dalarun's and moving in quite
different directions. Some scholars concentrate closely on one aspect of Robert's several pursuits; others offer a more global interpretation of his life. For clarity's sake, analytical emphases can be
divided into categories—gendered, institutional, eremitic, evangelical, psychological, and social—but summaries of scholars' work
(for which the reader can find full references in the bibliography)
show that there is considerable overlap among these approaches
and that any one interpretation can draw on several of them.

The simplistic "proto-feminist" interpretation, derived ultimately from Michelet, has undergone transformation. Already in
1978, Jacqueline Smith argued that Robert played a relatively small
part in the success of the women-centered monastery of Fontevraud, and that its foundation was a detour from his desired life,

that of a solitary hermit in search of spiritual perfection, and a di-
version from his most important mission, the preaching of the
Gospel. Although not denying Robert's awareness of the difficulties of religious women in his time, Smith finds that he "certainly
did not consider them a priority in his chosen field of work" and
that "the depth of Robert's concern for women . . . is therefore to be
questioned." Other scholars, although they do not identify Robert
as a precocious feminist, continued to consider Fontevraud central
to interpreting Robert's career and ideologies. Penny Schine Gold,
writing at the same time Dalarun completed this book, considered
Robert and his foundation in light of obstacles to female religious
vocation around 1100. Gold points out that Fontevraud and its
daughter houses were quite intentionally established as a monastic
order for religious women. Robert's plan, to integrate men formally into the structure of these communities, was original. It expressed, in Gold's view, an idea of the complementary nature of the
genders and gender roles. This "male/female co-operation" was a
matter of reciprocity, balance, and good order dependent on the
properly gendered behavior of all concerned. A dimmer view is
that of Loraine Simmons, who saw Robert's view of gender roles as
producing in the end a community of two groups incapable of in-
teraction, producing a "proximity anxiety" that is reflected in the
architecture of Fontevraud's abbey church.

Less focused on the details of arrangements of religious life
at Fontevraud than with locating it within patterns of monastic
foundation for women, the translator of this book saw Robert as
a standard-bearer, if not quite a proto-feminist. Robert, as I explained it, was perhaps the most prominent of a group of hermit-
preachers, who, along with patron bishops like Peter of Poitiers and
modest nobles like the lords who founded Fontevraud, sponsored
women's spiritual vocations and founded monasteries on their behalf. In this view, Robert's concern for female religious seekers and

his sponsorship of successful and even wealthy monasteries for women made his concern and guidance a sort of model for the multiplication of nunneries in twelfth-century France and England.

How important women and Fontevraud were in the trajectory of Robert's life, then, remains unresolved. Dalarun thought both central to understanding Robert. Other aspects of Robert's career, though, have taken precedence in the work of different scholars. Jean-Marc Bienvenu had only recently published the first full-length modern study of Robert of Arbrissel when Dalarun's book appeared. Bienvenu's extremely thorough research across many years led him to conclude that Robert was above all a late convert to the apostolic life, a practicing advocate of voluntary poverty, and a famed popular preacher. It is perhaps the eremitic aspect of Robert's many endeavors that Bienvenu stresses most. Fontevraud was for him, as for Smith, a detour that has become the focal point because of its great success and prestige long after Robert's death. Robert was, as Bienvenu has it, a "founder soon thrust aside," whose final constitution of Fontevraud as a traditional monastery came at "the hour of forced choices." Robert's story is thus somewhat melancholy: a true original, a free spirit, was eventually pinned down and obliged to adhere to the norms of the Church to which he belonged. In a book on Fontevraud's English priories, Berenice Kerr begins with a chapter on Robert, whom she says must be considered first as a preacher: "His eremiticism was a preparation for and a function of his call to be a preacher." In that sense, then, Robert's story ends tragically: the brothers of Fontevraud clothed his body for burial in the garb of a hermit preacher, but he was ultimately buried in the priestly vestments not in the cemetery of Fontevraud with his fellow seekers, as he had begged on his deathbed, but inside the abbey church, next to the high altar.

Less tragic in its connotations and less focused on Fontevraud or the women in Robert's entourage is a recent article by Alexandru Cizek that takes up Dalarun's remarks about how something of Robert's psychology is visible in the sources for his life. Cizek focuses on Robert's personality, in particular his roles as psychagogue, a guide of souls, and as the director of his own martyrdom. The perspective is that of twentieth-century psychoanalysis and social psychology: Robert's case reflects "the inexpiable struggle the ego must pursue in order to tame the unconscious" and his program of penitential spirituality aims toward "a collective anesthesia of sexual instinct." At the same time, Robert undergoes an "existential journey"; his career is one of increasing compromise with the reality of authority, a progression toward agreement with some of his critics, and the eventual retraction of some aspects of his spiritual project. In this view, Robert remains internally committed to his desire to guide and suffer martyrdom while allowing external manifestations, in particular the organization of Fontevraud, to reflect a reckoning with the realities of power and order. In the end, then, it is difficult if not impossible to reconcile all the various aspects and stages of Robert's career, and he remains an ambiguous if not wholly enigmatic figure.

Working from another direction, Daniel Pichot has also looked at the inner and outer Robert of Arbrissel, in particular the contrast of Robert as a solitary and Robert as a man operating in a crowd. The terms of discussion are, again, those of our times, with Robert undergoing a "crisis of consciousness," his personality, however embedded in its medieval world, also heralding "the beginnings of modernity." Pichot draws Robert as a man of paradox: his founding of institutions, first La Roë and then Fontevraud and its ancillary communities, must be understood not as a personal acceptance of formalized religious life. At the same time, his rejection of the world is not the same as rejection of his fellow humans. Robert's way, then, is a sort of rugged individualism, revealing a sense of self in relation to individuals and groups he encountered and attracted, ironically, with his commitment to the life of a hermit. "Secluded life and public life alternated and interpenetrated in undividable fashion."

The public and social aspects of Robert's career, then, continue to attract the attention of scholars. The question of Robert's mission to prostitutes has loomed large in consideration of his life, especially on the part of the moralistic judges of Robert, pro and con. After careful review of the medieval sources and modern discussions of Robert starting in the seventeenth century, Karen Green concludes that there is insufficient evidence Robert included any significant number of prostitutes in his following. Turning from Robert's followers to his patrons, W. Scott Jessee asks how so idiosyncratic a figure avoided the taint of heresy that attached to contemporaries of similar bent. A large part of the answer, Jessee finds, is the protection accorded across decades by members of the nobility of Anjou, up to and including the family of the counts. As a reforming archpriest in Rennes, a student in Angers, a hermit in the forest of Craon, a founder of La Roë, Fontevraud, and other communities, and a mentor for women, Robert interacted continually with powerful aristocrats and benefitted from their protection. His message may have been more moderate than his behavior, and his respect for ecclesiastical authority was always evident. In the end, though, patronage of powerful families in Anjou kept Robert, albeit subject to criticism, safe from official condemnation.

In 2001, the 900th anniversary of the foundation of Fontevraud, a group of scholars under the direction of Jacques Dalarun and Pierre Toubert gathered for a broad-ranging discussion of Robert of Arbrissel and his world. The results were published in 2004 and show that Robert continues to inspire new research and new interpretation. François-Olivier Touati argues that Robert, very much in tune with increased contact with the holy places of the East through pilgrimage and crusade, consciously created Fontevraud as a new Jerusalem, with various places within the complex dedicated to the Virgin, St. John the Evangelist, Lazarus, and Mary Magdalene, all of them associated with Christ's Passion. Dominique Barthélemy notes Robert's ban on his followers' involvement in the ordeal, a medieval judicial practice involving physical tests like picking up a hot iron or participating in a duel meant to show the judgment of God and therefore the truth of any matter. No other monastic pioneer of his age made any such prohibition, which turns out to have been in keeping with an abrupt turn away from the ordeal as a means of protecting monastic property in the Loire Valley at the dawn of the twelfth century. Robert emerges as a man very much of his time, well aware of the rhythms of his age, in these latest investigations.

Reformer, hermit, preacher, teacher, founder, penitent, mentor, patron, and protégé—Robert of Arbrissel is one or more of these things, in various combinations, to those who study him. In this book, the author remarks that Robert is an "auberge espagnol," a site from which what you take away depends in large part on what you bring. To reprise the idiom of psychology, Robert might also be a Rorschach blot, an intricate silhouette in which different observers might see any number of figures. The same figure might also look different at different times: Dalarun himself has recently observed that perhaps by focusing so intently on spirituality (as in this book), he has underestimated the unique opportunity Robert offered to women in his entourage, especially via Fontevraud. The questions recur and multiply, given the multifaceted nature of Robert's life and depending upon what aspect any one interpreter chooses to highlight. The element of mystery remains. Was Robert's life a tragic trajectory of compromise, making him a victim of the centralizing tendencies of his time? Or is the story one of insistent clinging to the charge to preach and teach that Robert managed until just days before his death? Is it appropriate or helpful to think of Robert as a precursor of modernity? If there is, as Dalarun asserts, no one truth about Robert of Arbrissel, then what is the use of subjective interpretations? Certainly any look at Robert must begin, as Dalarun does, with careful consideration of the sources of his life. Those are now available in English translation and cited in the notes here. Curious readers can also ponder other interpretations of Robert like those discussed above. In that way, others will continue the project Jacques Dalarun undertakes here: to understand who Robert was, what his life meant, and what the answers to those questions imply about his world and, just possibly, our own.

ABBREVIATIONS

AASS   *Acta sanctorum quotquot toto orbe coluntur.* 68 volumes. Antwerp, 1634 (reprinted Brussels, 1965–1970)

PL   *Patrologia cursus completus. Series latina.* Edited by J.-P. Migne. 221 volumes. Paris, 1844–1864

Both these massive collections of medieval source material have been digitized and are available for electronic access in many college and university libraries.

Robert of Arbrissel

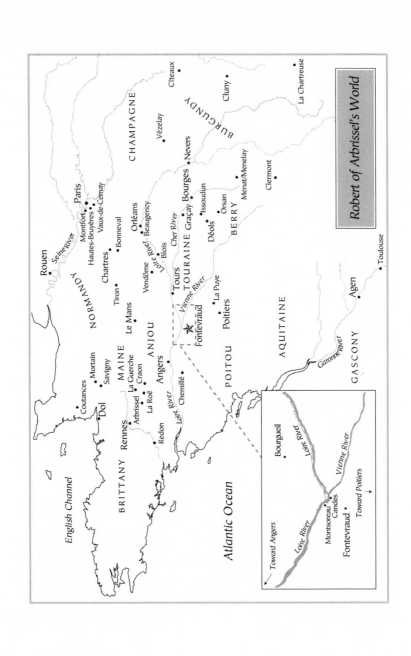

Robert of Arbrissel's World

1

TO THE SOURCES

Religious orders usually boast about their founders. The Order of Fontevraud kept obstinately silent about its own. This strange monastic federation—in which men were subordinated to women; which included some 150 priories in France, England, and Spain; and whose least exalted abbess was still the cousin of a prince or a king—preferred to forget Robert of Arbrissel, the medieval hermit to whom it owed its existence.

THE PLACES

Fontevraud lies near the confluence of the Loire and Vienne Rivers, a few miles to the south. From a distance, the abbey displays its splendor: the largest ensemble of religious architecture from the Ancien Régime.[1] The soft white of stone and the grey of roof-slates give the buildings their unity. Romanesque vaults, Renaissance cloister, and seventeenth-century lodge come into harmonious tranquility. Everything is in order.[2]

At the doorstep of the abbey church, Notre-Dame du Grand-

1. "Ancien Régime" is how historians refer to the period before the French Revolution of 1789.
2. Fontevraud's complex of buildings includes a twelfth-century church, dormitory, and kitchen, as well as numerous other structures built in later periods. Now fully restored, it is a tourist attraction and a cultural center hosting scholarly conferences.

Moutier ("Our Lady of the Great Monastery"), the fissures begin to appear. One look reveals the destiny of Fontevraud and Robert of Arbrissel; the whole story is written there in stone. The nave is broad, heavy, and somber, crowned with a heavy cover of four successive domes, at the end of which arises a gleaming choir. That eastern part of the church, including apse and transept, dates to the beginning of the twelfth century, contemporary with the founder. The nave dates to the years 1125–1150, when Petronilla of Chemillé, the first abbess, supervised its construction. Exceedingly wide and lacking side aisles, the nave calls to mind a palace chamber more than a church. Just as this Romanesque space is anchored firmly to earth, so is the choir (although older) celestial in its upright brightness. You sense already in flower there the transcendence that sprouted a few decades later at Saint-Denis, Laon, Senlis, Noyon, and Paris.[3] Napoleon's men made no mistake when, in 1804, they transformed the nave into a prison dormitory three stories high (a princely space logically turned into a jail), while leaving the choir intact in tribute to its very indomitability.[4]

Far from the Loire Valley, to the northwest via traces of long

3. The abbey church of Fontevraud is a late and impressive example of the Romanesque architectural style. The other churches to which Dalarun refers are among the first Gothic structures of the Middle Ages. This style had its origins at the monastery of Saint-Denis, just north of Paris, in the 1140s, just at the time the church of Fontevraud was completed.

4. That is, the nave, a much more "secular" structure, was put to a new use by the representatives of a new political regime. They did not dare, however, to modify the more spiritually evocative choir built in Robert's lifetime. On the abbey church and the entire complex of buildings at Fontevraud as they existed in the twelfth century, see Daniel Prigent, "Le cadre de vie à Fontevraud dans la seconde moitié du XIIᵉ siècle," *Fontevraud: Histoire-Archéologie* 5 (1997–1998): 39–56, which includes many illustrations and idem, "Fontevraud au début du XIIᵉ siècle: Les premiers temps d'une communauté monastique," in Jacques Dalarun, ed., *Robert d'Arbrissel et la vie religieuse dans l'Ouest de la France* (Turnhout, 2004), 255–279. For numerous images of the twelfth-century buildings on the site, see http://vrcoll.fa. pitt.edu/medart/image/France/fontevrault-new/fontvrlt-general.htm.

gone forests, is Arbrissel (or Arbressec) in Brittany, Robert's birth-place. There, in the little church of a vanished village, granite reigns supreme: sharp angles, no laciness, and little adornment other than grimacing stone crows, like poorly done sketches of some Aztec divinity. It was in this village, in this very church with its sense of ageless depths coming to the surface, that Robert was the parish priest.[5]

Places speak, especially in the Middle Ages. To name a man is to name a land. The identity of beings is in the soil where they are or where they remain. Robert of *Arbrissel,* founder of *Fontevraud:* born in the one place, buried in the other. On this journey from the fringes of Brittany to the borders of Poitou and Anjou, there are clues for understanding the most hidden itineraries.[6]

THE SOURCES

To proceed beyond intuition, the feel of places, it is necessary to go to the texts. Robert of Arbrissel had two Lives. That is, two narratives, two *vitae,* bear witness to his existence.[7] Without them and a few letters addressed to him, Robert would be nothing but a name at the bottom of documents, mentioned in a few chronicles, a grain of sand on the shores of history. Thanks to these two ac-counts, he is more than that. Historians have sufficient material to discuss Robert and quarrel about him. They have not refrained from doing so.

5. The small parish church of Arbrissel, in the Romanesque style like Fontevraud, also survives. Its modesty and eccentricity are, Dalarun finds, far more fitting a memorial to Robert than the grand abbey church of Fontevraud. It is ap-proximately eighty miles from Arbrissel to Fontevraud.

6. Anjou and Poitou are two regions of western France, the former north of the Loire River and with its center in the city of Angers, the latter south of the Loire with its capital at Poitiers.

7. *Vita,* literally "life," is the medieval Latin term for a biography of a holy per-son, often recognized as a saint.

The first Life, written shortly after Robert's death in 1116, is the work of Baudri.[8] For more than twenty-five years, Baudri was abbot of the monastery of Saint-Pierre of Bourgueil, which faced Fontevraud from the right bank of the Loire in eastern Anjou. In 1107, after a few unsuccessful attempts, Baudri raised himself to the archiepiscopal throne at Dol in Brittany. The triumph was short-lived. Amidst his flock, Archbishop Baudri considered himself "among scorpions," surrounded by their "brutal ferocity."[9] Following a path reversing Robert's, from the Loire Valley to Brittany, the archbishop's literary interests changed. Abandoning composition of the elegant court poetry for which he had become well known, Baudri threw himself into hagiography.[10] In 1116, he was over seventy, having attained unexpected old age. Once past his biblical three score and ten, the archbishop dreamed of performing pious works. Petronilla, the abbess of Fontevraud, asked him for one. At her request, Baudri wrote a biography of the founder, from birth to death. The narrative is short, in rather grandiose Latin— Baudri's literary reputation demanded it be so. The *vita* surveys the major stages of Robert's life: changes of situation, changes of place. However, it is somewhat more than a *curriculum vitae* or a work-on-demand. Some unexpected connections between the court poet and the hermit make themselves known. At times, the narrative examines Robert's soul, his torments, in quick, penetrating glances.

To complete this first narrative, and also to correct it, Petronilla of Chemillé felt the need for a second Life.[11] She commissioned

8. Baudri of Dol, *Vita Prima B. Roberti de Arbrissello* [*First Life of Robert of Arbrissel*] in *Patrologia cursus completus, Series Latina*, ed. J.-P. Migne, 221 vols. (Paris 1844–1864; hereafter PL) 162: 1043–1058; English translation in Bruce L. Venarde, *Robert of Arbrissel: A Medieval Religious Life* (Washington, DC, 2004), 6–21.

9. These phrases occur in Baudri, *First Life*, section 2 (PL 162: 1045; Venarde, *Robert of Arbrissel*, 8).

10. "Hagiography" is the general term for writings about holy people.

11. Andreas of Fontevraud, *Vita Altera B. Roberti de Arbrissello* [*Second Life of Robert of Arbrissel*] in PL 162: 1057–1078 (sections 1–42) and Jacques Dalarun,

it from a man whom the distinctive statutes of Fontevraud placed under her control and allegiance: the brothers' prior, Andreas. At least that is the received wisdom, since the narrative itself is anonymous, its hypothetical attribution passed down the ages. Longer than Baudri's account, this second *vita* recounts only the last six months of Robert's life, but in minute detail; not one sigh of mortal agony goes unmentioned. Above all, the narrative is an opportunity to record the master's last wishes, in particular those concerning the governance of the Order of Fontevraud. Petronilla was counting on it. She expected a record upon which she could base the legitimacy of her power as never before.

The reader should not be surprised, though, that some of the material in this second Life comes from Middle French, in the vocabulary of the fifteenth and sixteenth centuries. This is a lovely language, not quite the same as modern French; it takes on added grace from its exoticism. Composed only two or three years after the death of Fontevraud's founder, and so originally in Latin, part of Andreas's text survives only in a more recent translation into Middle French.[12]

In contrast to the edifying *vitae*, two letters addressed to Robert contain no flattery. The first, written in the final years of the eleventh century, comes from Bishop Marbode of Rennes. The second, dating to the first years of the twelfth century, is the work of Geoffrey, abbot of La Trinité in Vendôme. Both were men of consequence, among the most eminent of the secular and regular clergy.[13] Their letters are indictments. Robert is accused of taking

---

L'impossible sainteté: La Vie retrouvée de Robert d'Arbrissel (v. 1045–1116), fondateur de Fontevraud (Paris, 1985), 284–299 (sections 42–75); English translation in Venarde, *Robert of Arbrissel*, 26–67.

12. Dalarun himself discovered the French version, written ca. 1500, of the second Life in a manuscript preserved in the French National Library in Paris but unknown to previous scholars. The full *vita* contains about forty percent more material than is preserved in Latin.

13. Marbode of Rennes (ca. 1035–1123), like Baudri a noted poet, was for

pleasure in the company of women and upsetting the social order. His cardinal sin is not lust, though; it is the gravest of all, the sin of pride so prominent in this feudal age. It is the presumptuousness of a man who thinks himself stronger than his enemy and tumbles headlong into his snares.

The reader will also find along the way a few other texts of lesser importance, but the essence of Robert's life is in these four sources, two Lives and two letters. Each pair facing the other, they outline the characteristic traits of the dossier on Robert: conflict and contradiction. There is praise and blame, but Robert does not elicit a lukewarm response.

THE STORY

Historians have not escaped Robert's spell. Pulled this way and that, understood more in the service of other assertions than studied for himself, the founder of Fontevraud constitutes a sizeable interpretive stake. But the subject is what the French call an "auberge espagnol," a Spanish inn: everybody finds in it what he brings to it. Historians of communist Eastern Europe saw in Robert's social message an expression of popular yearning to stem the injustice of the social order.[14] Michelet, in a famous page of *The Middle Ages*, explored other paths of interpretation. In his eyes,

---

many years director of the cathedral school in Angers. Elected bishop of Rennes in Brittany in 1096, Marbode wrote his letter to Robert shortly thereafter. Geoffrey of Vendôme (ca. 1070–1132) had already been abbot of his Benedictine house for nearly fifteen years when he wrote to Robert in 1106. Marbode was a member of the "secular clergy," that is, those living in the world and charged with the care of souls, whereas Geoffrey was one of the "regular clergy," those living under a *regula*, a monastic rule, separated from the world. Full references to text and translation of both letters are in chapter 3 below.

14. The reference is to a study of Robert of Arbrissel and other wandering preachers by the East German scholar Ernst Werner, *Pauperes Christi: Studien zu sozial-religiösen Bewegungen im Zeitalter des Reformpapsttums* (Leipzig, 1956).

Robert was above all a defender of the weaker sex: "He reopened Christ's breast to women."[15] The idea took off. Instead of somber, nightmarish centuries, some people today conceive of the Middle Ages as a dream world, one too beautiful to be true, onto which our age projects its desires—just as others once projected their fears and repulsion onto Gothic darkness. Robert is a somewhat sappy hero of this imagined world; the foundation of Fontevraud becomes a courtly undertaking directed at noble ladies. As to the founder, even if like his followers he wore an outfit "worthy of the hippies of our times," fear not: Régine Pernoud assures us that Robert "led a life of perfect chastity among this diverse crowd."[16]

Popular yearning or the liberation of women? The chapters that follow do not pretend to settle these great debates. The reader will not find out here for certain if Robert slept amidst his disciples of both sexes in all chaste honor, because nowhere is the matter settled in the texts. Nor is there much in this book about the institution of Fontevraud, its juridical organization, and the rapid growth of its wealth. Charters, bulls, and statutes will detain us less than the narrative sources.[17]

15. The great patriotic French historian Jules Michelet (1798–1874) wrote a multivolume history of his country, including much on the Middle Ages. The quotation is from Jules Michelet, *Œuvres complètes* (Paris, 1971–1982), 4: 459.

16. Régine Pernoud, *Women in the Days of the Cathedrals*, translated and adapted by Anne Côté-Harriss (San Francisco, 1998), 115–116.

17. A charter (*carta*) is the medieval term for any written document, but the word usually refers to a legal agreement, often concerning property. The charters mentioned here record donations to the abbey of Fontevraud, many hundreds of which survive; those written before his death often include the name of Robert of Arbrissel. A full modern edition of Fontevraud charters is *Grand Cartulaire de Fontevraud*, ed. Jean-Marc Bienvenu et al. (Poitiers, 2000–). "Bull," named for the lead seal (*bulla*) attached to confirm a document's authenticity, here refers to documents issued by the popes in Rome, who confirmed the list of estates owned by Fontevraud at regular intervals in the twelfth century. Statutes were in the Middle Ages (as now) collections of regulations; Robert of Arbrissel dictated a set for Fontevraud shortly before his death (see chapter 5 below).

This book tells a story of torment, the tale of a man prey to the flame and who, desperately alone, sought the means to extinguish the fire that scorched him from within. It was a long, hard road, passing from contempt for the world to the reconciliation of the spirit and the flesh, from obsession with error to the approach of grace. In the sources we can hear for a moment people of another age as they talk. They speak not of liberation but of salvation. The narrative, relying on the sources, is a sort of "Life of a Saint"—and thus relies not only on the *vitae* by Baudri and Andreas, but also on the accusatory letters from Marbode and Geoffrey. The saint attracts our attention from afar. He is a *lucifer*, a bearer of light, and such a figure never passes without scandal. In our times, to whom will occur the hope, even the idea, of being canonized? The measured steps of the Congregation of Rites, a weighty, centralizing, and deliberate apparatus, postpone to a distant future the dreams of possible candidates for the altars.[18] At the dawn of the twelfth century, whoever elicited discussion—preferably (but not necessarily) in complimentary terms—and whoever showed virtue a little out of the ordinary could hope to pass away "in the odor of sanctity."[19]

Robert of Arbrissel was among those who one day fixed on the project of being a saint. Pride, ever and always? Well, a saint does not attract attention only to himself. Just like the finger of John the Baptist pointed at Christ, Robert attracts attention in order to direct it elsewhere.[20] Robert's presumption presupposes humility, and

18. The process of saint-making was gradually formalized in Robert's lifetime and thereafter. In the early Middle Ages (ca. AD 500–1000), saints emerged from local cults, without any regular or centralized procedure. In the twelfth century, however, the revitalized papacy began to take control of the process of canonization, which eventually became the long, complex, and bureaucratic process centered in Rome that it remains today. The Congregation of Rites, established in 1588, changed its name to the Congregation for the Causes of Saints in 1969.

19. The "odor of sanctity" is an ancient idea referring to the special atmosphere holy people created around them. It could also refer literally to a sweet smell said to be emitted by the corpses of the holy dead.

20. In the Gospel of Matthew 3:11–12, John the Baptist performed his rite of

his will prepared the way for his surrender. On the roads of western France, naked he followed the naked Christ.[21]

purification by water while pointing out that one far more powerful than he was to come, pointing the way to Jesus Christ.

21. Another old Christian expression, referring to the poverty of Jesus and His care for the poor that came to be associated with the apostolic life of some medieval religious people and their conscious imitation of Christ's first disciples and the early church.

2

FLESH AND THE WORD

BEGINNINGS

Robert of Arbrissel was born around 1045—or at least historians say so, on slender evidence. Did he himself know the date of his birth? Probably not, and this kind of detail, furthermore, did not interest hagiographers at all.[1] The true birth of a saint is at the other end of the story; the day of his death, of the return to his Father, of his deliverance, becomes the saint's feast day. What we call being born was, in medieval spirituality, nothing but the beginning of an earthly exile, a night always too long.

On the other hand, we know very well where he came from. In concentric circles, Baudri of Bourgueil narrows down the place of Robert's origin: he was born in Christendom, in Lower Brittany, in the territory of Rennes, at Arbrissel—very much on the margins.[2] Arbrissel is on the eastern fringe of Brittany, a few steps from Anjou, in one of those places that is even now at the boundary of departments, after having been for centuries at the boundary of dioceses and provinces, and which, given its location between more settled areas, longer than elsewhere preserved the remains of great

---

1. That is, those who wrote about the lives and activities of saints.

2. Unless otherwise noted, the material cited and quoted in this chapter comes from portions of the two *vitae*: Baudri, *First Life*, sections 7–18 (PL 162: 1046–1053; Venarde, *Robert of Arbrissel*, 10–16), and Andreas, *Second Life*, sections 40–41 (PL 162: 1077–1078; Venarde, *Robert of Arbrissel*, 49–50).

forests.[3] Robert was a native and *colonus*, that is, a legally free small-holder. The hagiographer adds that he was the "son of a priest, born of a clerical family," something quite unremarkable in this eleventh-century world. Monks were held to a vow of chastity, but the Church had not yet sought systematically to impose the celibate life on its secular priests, its parish clergy. Therefore, this was an ordinary situation in the mid-eleventh century but not, at least officially, when Baudri wrote his account around the year 1117.[4] His discomfort is conspicuous. Concerning Robert's parents, Damalioch and Orguende, Baudri provides names but adds not a word boasting of their merits. Such silence is meaningful in light of hagiographical tradition and its commonplaces. In saints' Lives, parents are always very noble, even nobler in heart than in blood. The hero is thus from the first both a saint and of good stock; doubly predestined, he requires only the nuisance of being born. Robert, though, did not have these gifts at the cradle. His sanctity was wholly to be earned, to be won. At death's door, he would recall that he was "born of a little old man and a poor little woman." In the village of Arbrissel, the pastor was hardly distinguishable from his flock, like them attached to the land from which he earned his subsistence. He was at least less poor and better educated, but that meant little. Like his flock he submitted to a patron, the lord of L'Epine, and beyond him the powerful lord of La Guerche who held this corner of Brittany under his sway. Robert was sent to

3. Modern France is divided into numerous administrative districts called departments; Arbrissel is in the department of Ille-et-Vilaine but within 10 miles of the borders of three other departments. In medieval terms, Arbrissel was on the border between Brittany and Anjou and at the edge of dioceses centered at Rennes and Angers.

4. One goal of religious reform emanating from Rome from the mid-eleventh century forward was the imposition of celibacy on all Christian clergy. Such was the theoretical norm by the time Robert died, an enormous ideological change that corresponds almost exactly to his lifetime.

neighboring towns to gather the minimal knowledge fitting to a priest's son. He went from one place to another, unsatisfied, and Baudri suggests, to use an old pun, that he pursued his studies but did not succeed in catching up with them.

After his father's death, Robert would naturally take his place in this slightly out-of-the-way parish of Arbrissel. Just as naturally, he would have married. No narrative source is explicit about either point, but I assume both for good reasons. In 1127, a council held at Nantes forbade the priests of Brittany from bequeathing their benefices to their sons,[5] but half a century earlier there would have been no question about Damalioch's successor. If his son had in turn taken a wife, it would have been just as his ancestors had done. Fathers hoped to pass along these little benefices—so much more precious for being meager. In the case of Robert, the sources give a few indications in support of the suspicion that he married. Baudri assures us that his hero embraced chastity "insofar as he was able." Given the spotless catalogue of virtues that the Life of a saint was meant to be, such a qualification is quite meaningful. Marbode of Rennes suggested that by holding himself back from temptation amid a crowd of women, Robert was trying to expiate, thirty years later, an old sin of a similar type.

Testimony from the *vita* of one of Robert's companions, Bernard of Tiron, gives a vivid account of the behaviors and mentalities of the period.

At that time, it was the custom in Normandy that priests took wives openly, that they celebrated marriage, siring sons and daughters to whom they left churches after their deaths by hereditary right. They married off daughters and often, if they had no other property, gave them a church as dowry. When they took wives, before joining them-

---

5. Here "benefice" refers to ecclesiastical office plus the landed property associated with it. The council of churchmen at Nantes, then, objected to the process of passing down both position and land that did not belong to a family but to the Church.

selves to them they vowed in the parents' presence that they would never abandon them. In doing so they obliged themselves by oath never to
cease being fornicators, never to approach the body and blood of Christ
other than guiltily and unworthily, and in thus approaching while guilty,
to eat and drink their own damnation.[6]

This last sentence testifies to a different vision, another culture.
From their own point of view, the practice of the Norman priests is
perfectly logical and the writer, in spite of his disapproval, knew
how to present its coherence: priests held parishes as hereditary
benefices. Like peasant holdings, this patrimony risked fragmenta-
tion because partible inheritance was customary in families; this
was a practice different from that of the strategy of the rich, who
by this time sought to pass on family property to one son. The
joining of spouses, on the other hand, went forward for clerical
marriages as for all others; the heart of this text is about marriage
in due form, celebrated publicly with oaths of fidelity, based on the
agreement of all parties and mutual consent—specifically, the consent of the man and the woman's family.

Robert would have joined this clerical social order just at the
moment it began to falter. However, if he did not reconcile the married state and the priesthood for long, it was for other reasons. On
his deathbed, he accused himself of having "fallen into the crime of
simony in the election of a certain bishop of Rennes." Simony was
the mingling of money and religion, in particular the sale of sacra-
ments or traffic in ecclesiastical offices.[7] The historian Jean-Marc

6. Bernard of Tiron, like Robert of Arbrissel a preacher and monastic founder,
was born about the same time in Picardy and died only a few weeks after Robert, in
the spring of 1116. See Bernard Beck, *Saint Bernard de Tiron: l'ermite, le moine et le
monde* (Cormelles-le-Royal, 1998). The quotation is from the *vita* of Bernard written ca. 1135–ca. 1140 by a monk of Tiron known as Geoffrey the Fat, edited and
with a French translation in ibid., 366–369 (section 51). Latin text also in PL 172:
1397.

7. Simony is so called after Simon the Magus, who tried to buy from St. Peter
the power of the Holy Spirit to work miracles (Acts 8:9–24).

Bienvenu considered that Robert had sinned this way in 1076, in the election of Sylvester de La Guerche to the episcopal throne. For it was necessary to overlook several matters to make such a person a prelate: Sylvester was a sword-bearing illiterate who had never been ordained as a priest. Nevertheless, the parish of Arbrissel was under his ultimate authority; Robert was his subordinate and client. These ties obliged Robert to work in Sylvester's favor. In 1078, a legate[8] of Pope Gregory VII deposed this odd excuse for a bishop. Robert, Bienvenu proposed, had to flee Brittany soon after, tarred with the same brush as his patron.[9]

Robert took up his studies again in Paris. The university that would be the city's glory did not yet exist—far from it—but already schools flourished on the Ile de la Cité.[10] Robert arrived in Paris a simoniac and doubtless a nicolaite. (This ecclesiastical term designates clerics who live in the "sin of the flesh." If our hero was a nicolaite, it was in the same way that Monsieur Jourdain spoke prose—without knowing it.[11]) By the time he departed, he had become the bitter enemy of both simony and nicolaism. Baudri says little of this sojourn except that Robert's zeal for study and austere conduct grew all the while. As if to underline the importance of the

8. Legates were papal ambassadors, used increasingly from the eleventh century forward as the popes' way of asserting their authority over the whole of Catholic Christendom.

9. Jean-Marc Bienvenu, *L'étonnant fondateur de Fontevraud: Robert d'Arbrissel* (Paris, 1981), 20–21.

10. The Ile de la Cité is the island in the Seine River that then, as now, was the center of Paris; only recently, in Robert's time, had major settlement begun on the adjacent river banks to the north and south of the island.

11. Nicolaites are mentioned in Revelations 2:6 and 2:15, but almost nothing is known of the beliefs of this early Christian sect. Their association with clerical marriage is a much later development. For a rural priest of the mid-eleventh century, the idea that clerical marriage was *ipso facto* sinful would have come as a surprise, just as Monsieur Jourdain, the title character in Molière's play *Le bourgeois gentilhomme* (1670), is taken aback to discover that he has been speaking prose for over forty years without knowing it.

stay in Paris, Baudri placed it in historical time, during the reign of King Philip I (hence 1060–1108) and Pope Gregory VII (1073–1085): "I speak thus to indicate clearly the era in which Robert studied and grew up." The reference to Gregory VII is more than just a simple marker of time, for it is an indication of the atmosphere that the longtime student imbibed. In the teaching of the schoolmasters, discussions among fellow students, and sermons here and there, the ecclesiastical reform underway always held a prominent place.

Since the dawn of the eleventh century, an increasingly powerful current of reform had flowed across Christendom. For those who desired to renew the Church, two practices seemed particularly unacceptable: the hold of the lay aristocracy over Church property and offices and clerical concubinage or sexual indulgence. The guardianship of the Breton lords of L'Epine and La Guerche over the parish of Arbrissel and the marriage in due form of Norman priests (it was the reformers who spoke of these arrangements as "concubinage") provide examples of this state of affairs. Such practices shaped the Church from top to bottom. In 1073, the archdeacon Hildebrand, who for a long while had been a guiding force for reform, was elected pope under the name of Gregory VII. Already the next year a Roman synod[12] proclaimed the degeneracy of simoniac and nicolaite priests and invited the faithful to desert the churches of disobedient priests. Papal legates tried to enforce these decrees everywhere, not without resistance. A Paris synod in 1074 rejected the notion of clerical celibacy, which it deemed contrary to reason and human nature. We must imagine, then, a Breton student falling into the middle of such debates almost as if from another planet.[13]

"Behold: I was conceived in wickedness and nurtured in sin

12. A synod is a gathering of ecclesiastical officials to discuss any matters of Christian thought or practice.

13. For an account of the early stages of the revolution that in fact preceded

and I have sinned by my own fault in countless ways." Is this final confession of Robert's, as reported by Andreas, to be understood as a supreme gesture of humility from a serene soul—or should it be taken literally? This priest, blemished by simony and concubinage, thought himself the antithesis of a saint. Instead of the quasi-immaculate conception of legendary Christian heroes, he was marked from birth with the stamp of sin. That the two *vitae* concur on this point justifies taking this final confession at face value. Baudri hints at Robert's torment: "In him there was a kind of internal conflict, a roaring of the mind, a groaning from the guts that one could find cruel and impious; it was susceptible to no cure and many murmured that it was excessive, above and beyond miserable human frailty." Later on, in the time of Fontevraud's glory, the era of success and fame, Baudri reports that "when he was thought the calm in the crowd, the master was alone consumed with anguish."[14]

There is great significance to a twelfth-century torment that is almost anachronistic in its modernity. What we would call personal psychological makeup bursts forth in public display in other contemporary texts. Individuals in these documents are not torn between two feelings or choices but instead are passive participants in a battle between a gang of demons and a legion of angels. Medieval psychology, then, is a spectator sport: it is *psychomachia*, a contest for a soul, a duel between forces which, seen from afar, transcend the individual concerned.[15] When Baudri speaks of internal conflict, of anguish—in a word, of interiority—his expression

Gregory, see Colin Morris, *The Papal Monarchy: The Western Church from 1050 to 1250* (Oxford, 1989), 101–113.

14. Baudri, *First Life*, section 22 (PL 1062: 1055); Venarde, *Robert of Arbrissel*, 19.

15. The notion of *psychomachia*, meaning "struggle in the soul," was best known to medieval readers through the poem of that name by Prudentius (348–ca. 405), who depicted the struggle of Christianity and paganism allegorically as a series of duels between virtues and vices.

rings true to us because it is at odds with that of the times. Baudri's pen hesitates; he writes *quidam singultus*, a certain hiccup, sob, or groan. Only with great difficulty does the vocabulary of psychology emerge from the subject matter.

Robert's consciousness of culpability is all the sharper because it came late. Only after the age of thirty did the Breton priest learn that he was a sinner, guilty of something he never suspected wrong, in which he was fixed, and in which, worse yet, he had been conceived. What emerges as a question of internal moral struggle brings into view far more than an individual crisis of conscience. In Robert's mind two cultures, two ways of being, confronted one another: the lot of generations of parish clergy versus the vision the Roman Church was trying to impose in the last quarter of the eleventh century. Acculturation did not happen without conflict and harm. A man renounced himself and regarded with horror a situation that previously had seemed to him the ordinary state of things. Robert's soul preserved the fracture this moral earthquake made in him, and from it proceeded the quest that he now undertook.

REFORMER

There is no convert more zealous than a recent one, so Robert must have burned to spread reform far and wide. The bishop of Rennes provided him with the opportunity. This was none other than Sylvester de La Guerche, restored to the position from which he had been deposed. Bishop Sylvester remained uncultured, a fact Baudri does not hide. The mitered nobleman, too, had been affected by the Gregorian requirements of which he had first fallen foul, producing a strange coincidence of two life paths that is symbolic of the mental revolution underway at the end of the eleventh century. Sylvester sought to surround himself with learned clerics to raise up the church of Rennes. Hearing Robert's merits praised, the bishop traveled to Paris to beg aid in his task. If the episode as Baudri recounts it is authentic, it speaks volumes about what an intellectual desert Brittany was at the time. Robert accepted the charge to help Sylvester put right his holy mother church of Rennes. Beyond the reform program that united the two men, other links doubtless played a role. Robert remained his patron's man. He could not very well refuse to help.

For four years, Robert was Sylvester's archpriest.[16] In effect, he ran the diocese. The one-time warrior, full of good intentions but clearly out of his depths, gave over the reins of power to the cleric polished with Parisian culture. "He was an utterly faithful patron of his bishop, both because the bishop was his patron and because he did not scorn Robert's patronage." Robert's strategy was straight out of the Gregorian playbook: "To free churches from shameful servitude to lay people and to put a stop to incestuous fornications by priests and lay people." For the Church worked not only to confine clergy to celibacy but also, by multiplying degrees of prohibited consanguinity, to push to its outer limits the definition of incestuous marriage and to suppress the polygamy still current, especially among the aristocracy.[17]

This vast program was bound to make innumerable enemies. Conflicts between reformers and adherents of the old marital order were of unprecedented intensity.[18] In 1114, Bishop Peter of Poitiers excommunicated Duke William IX of Aquitaine, called "the first

16. The duties attached to this title varied across time and space in the Middle Ages. Robert was evidently responsible for supervision of all priests in the diocese of Rennes.

17. In the eleventh century, the papacy sponsored new and far more restrictive calculations about the degree of kinship considered incestuous, increasing approximately twentyfold the likelihood that any given union would fall within prohibited boundaries. See R. I. Moore, *The First European Revolution, c. 970–1215* (Oxford, 2000), 92–94. The "polygamy" referred to here is more exactly resource polygyny. In the eleventh century, powerful men had not multiple wives but multiple recognized female sexual partners and dependents.

18. On the conflicts in the eleventh and twelfth centuries, see Georges Duby,

Troubadour." This prince flaunted his concubine, Viscountess Maubergeonne of Châtellerault, abandoning the bedchamber of his sole legitimate spouse as recognized by the Church. Was that the offense for which Peter condemned him? Perhaps. When Bishop Gerard of Angoulême, acting as papal legate, renewed the sanction, it was certainly for that reason. Gerard got off lightly, since William contented himself with jeering at the bishop's baldness: "Your hair will go curly before I renounce the countess." Peter of Poitiers was treated less mildly at the time of the original excommunication. As the chronicler William of Malmesbury tells it,

> When, Peter, the very holy bishop of Poitiers, openly admonished William and in face of his obstinacy began to excommunicate him publicly, the enraged duke grabbed the prelate by the hair and, brandishing his sword, cried out, "You will die if you do not absolve me!" The bishop first simulated fear to gain time, then boldly pronounced the end of the excommunication formula: he suspended the count from Christian society so that he would not dare to eat or even speak with anyone unless he repented at once. His duty done as he saw fit and eager for the crown of martyrdom, Peter offered his neck to the duke: "Go ahead, strike!" William, rallying and recovering his usual wit, replied, "I hate you so much that I will not honor you with my hatred and you will never enter heaven by my hand."[19]

In fact, the duke spared the bishop to better prolong his agony. Peter died on April 4, 1115, from ill-treatment suffered in prison and from the exile the count imposed on him.[20]

Warriors were the most violent opponents of the reformers;

The Knight, the Lady, and the Priest: The Making of Modern Marriage in Medieval France, trans. Barbara Bray (New York, 1983).

19. William of Malmesbury, *Gesta Regum Anglorum: The History of the English Kings*, ed. R. A. B. Mynors et al., 2 vols. (Oxford, 1998–1999), 1: 784–785 (section 439), translation altered slightly. The historian William of Malmesbury (ca. 1090–1143) was an English monk.

20. Bishop Peter was driven out of Poitiers, never to return because he steadfastly refused to lift the excommunication. On Peter and his career, see George T.

violence was their way of life. The clergy were not easily defeated, either. Bernard of Tiron learned the hard way when he attacked the matrimonial practices of the Norman clergy mentioned above. "He delivered some of them, but the greater part of them he was unable to save from hell."[21] Even taking into account the standard embellishment of hagiography, such an account renders few saved. Indeed, the disobedient defended themselves, trying to frighten Bernard and laying traps for him. The most fearsome adversaries were the wives, fearful of being separated from their priest-husbands. They tried to have the intruder killed. The women's rage is understandable. For them, busy with their children, repudiation would be the end of everything, since it was disaster, in this age, for a woman to live outside the power of a man, whether father, brother, or husband. When Bernard of Tiron preached at Coutances, there was "an archdeacon, with wife and children, accompanied by a great entourage of priests and clerics." The scene played out in the diocesan center, and the clergy gathered there to celebrate Pentecost were so numerous that the cathedral church could hardly hold them. This archdeacon, like Robert at Rennes, was the bishop's right-hand man, and spoke for the whole secular clergy of lower Normandy when he asked why Bernard, a monk and dead to the world, was preaching to the living. The preacher was, after all, a son of St. Benedict.[22] The encounter in Coutances poses a basic question: why did monks want to impose on other clergy, those who lived in the world, an order not their own, an or-

---

Beech, "Biography and the Study of 11th Century Society: Bishop Peter II of Poitiers (1087–1115)," *Francia* 7 (1979): 101–121.

21. The remainder of this paragraph and the next is drawn from Geoffrey the Fat, *Life of Bernard*, sections 51–54 (Beck, *Saint Bernard de Tiron*, 366–371; PL 172: 1397–1399).

22. Benedict of Nursia was the author of the most widely used monastic rule (see note 29 below). As a monk of the house of Saint-Cyprien in Poitiers, Bernard was his spiritual offspring.

der doubtless good for these recluses, dead to the world and already in heavenly light, but one that repelled the living in every fiber of their being?

Cornered, Bernard launched into a long and prolix discourse. Samson killed his enemies with the jawbone of an ass; in the same way Christ wards off evil by means of a man dead to the world, a tough jawbone that "chews the shell of Scripture to separate allegorical sense from tropological, to distinguish tropological sense from anagogical."[23] Bernard had to devise his reasoning on the spot. Was the archdeacon convinced? That is what the hagiographer would have us believe. In any case it was the archdeacon who calmed the crowd—not forgetting the wives—and spared Bernard from being gutted. This last stroke is revealing: Bernard was not up against a little group of hysterics or marginal people; the archdeacon acted out of his authority and the diocesan secular clergy stood behind him in good order—the order that the archdeacon defended.

After four years, Bishop Sylvester of Rennes died. The hatred of the Breton clergy for Robert could finally be unleashed. Without waiting to hear more, Robert fled to Angers. The old world was coming apart, but not without resistance. Robert had not managed to convey his desire for perfection to others and he wanted to atone for his failure. At Angers, where he arrived in 1093, he resumed his studies. More than anything else, though, reading and prayer were the antidote to *otium*, the idleness of vagabond daydreams in which the Enemy—that is, the "lures of the flesh"—more easily seizes a foothold. To subdue the urge, Robert spent two years in an iron tunic. Earlier in the century, deep in the valleys of the Apennines,

---

23. According to a widely understood scheme of interpretation alluded to by Bernard's biographer, the Bible is to be understood in four senses: the historical or literal, the allegorical (symbolic), the tropological (moral), and the anagogical (spiritual or mystical).

Dominic the Mailed, a zealous disciple of Peter Damian, had intro-
duced this garment.[24] The soul is in the body's prison; the intention
of the cuirass is to liberate the soul by imprisoning the body, putting it at the soul's mercy. The wearer thought more than ever of
the body. At the slightest movement, metal plates pinched the
trunk, the living bones. Robert wore fine clothing over this instrument of torture. Only God saw his merits. This secret lasted two
years. "Then the day came when Robert, renouncing the world,
took himself to the long desired wilderness."

<h3 style="text-align:center">HERMIT</h3>

Robert retained the traits of a hermit when he was remembered later on. This departure for the *eremum*, the "desert," was
thus a great moment in his life. It was what in that era people
called a "conversion"—not, as today, the entry into an entirely new
religion, but a turning point or rather a turnabout, a personal revolution. (Hagiographers usually dated events in saints' lives in terms
of the number of years after conversion.) Once the soul was relieved of this world's trifles, the convert hoped nothing but God
would dwell there. This was both an exceptional moment and an
ordinary move. There are, as it were, no *vitae* without such a departure for the desert or a substitute for it. Moreover, Baudri describes
his hero's decision as banal, expected, and inescapable.

The origin of this tradition lies in the Middle East. There the
desert is more than a dream or figure of speech—the rocky crags
beside the Red Sea or Lower Egypt's expanses of niter, "a white

24. St. Dominic Loricatus, "the Mailed," was born around 995. Ordained ille-
gally when his father bribed a bishop, Dominic decided to do penance for this act of
simony for the rest of his life by his uncomfortable clothing and extreme asceticism. He eventually became a hermit under the supervision of Peter Damian (on
whom see below) and continued his fierce acts of self-denial and self-punishment
until his death in about 1060.

mineral sea whose rigid crust is not susceptible to winds resounding under the feet in some places like a crystal dome."[25] To such inhospitable sites hermits of the fourth century departed to seek God: Anthony, Paul of Thebes, Pachomius, and the two named Macarius.[26] Regretting that they were unable to become martyrs in a now-Christian Roman Empire, they went out to encounter instead the physically unbearable. Their example spread far and wide. St. Jerome, Doctor of the Church and translator of the Vulgate Bible, was fascinated by these Egyptians and wrote a *vita* of Paul of Thebes while he himself had retreated to the desert of Calchis.[27] John Cassian, before he became archbishop of Marseilles, included in his *Conferences* the sayings of these men whose way of life he had shared for more than ten years.[28] St. Martin, evangelist to the Gauls, and Benedict, father of Western monasticism, complete a list of only the most famous saints who had their time, be it short or long, in the desert.[29]

25. Jacques Lacarrière, *Les hommes ivres de Dieu* (Paris, 1975), 9.

26. Saints Anthony, Paul of Thebes, Pachomius, Macarius the Elder, and Macarius the Younger lived as hermits and monks in Lower Egypt, all dying there between about AD 350 and 400.

27. St. Jerome (ca. 340–420), one of the so-called doctors (meaning "teachers," a title of great honor) of the late antique era, translated the Hebrew Old Testament and the Greek New Testament into the Latin version best known to the medieval West, the Vulgate Bible. One phase of Jerome's life was spent in desert retreat in Syria, where he wrote a sketch of Paul of Thebes. See Jerome, "Life of Paul of Thebes" in *Early Christian Lives*, trans. Carolinne White (New York, 1998), 71–84.

28. John Cassian (ca. 360–ca. 435) traveled around the Mediterranean before settling in Marseilles around 415. *The Conferences* recounts his conversations with Egyptian hermits about the pursuit of inner spiritual life and was widely read in medieval monasteries. In Marseilles, Cassian founded two monasteries, one for men and one for women, the latter the first nunnery in western Europe.

29. St. Martin of Tours (ca. 315–ca. 397) was a former Roman soldier and Christian convert who brought the life of spiritual retreat learned in the Mediterranean to western France and created a "Gallic Egypt" for followers in the Loire Valley. He was also a vigorous missionary preacher and ultimately became bishop of Tours. For comparisons of Robert and Martin, see below, chapter 5. St. Benedict

Ireland, too, was once a school for this eremitic ideal.[30] Some scholars think that by indirect influence of Celtic culture, Irish practices reached western France. This is very unlikely. None of the *vitae* of Robert's contemporaries refers to the compatriots of St. Patrick, whereas the example of the Egyptian hermits is present in their deeds. It should be noted that the Eastern Fathers had exceptional literary renown and that writing can transmit influence across centuries and from one end of the earth to another while everything oral gets lost and forgotten. The rather uniform accounts of Egyptian, Syrian, and Palestinian religious austerity (*vitae* of individuals, collections of sayings by the desert fathers, or reports by visitors like John Cassian) circulated whole or in parts, in Latin versions, across the West. In monasteries and schools these accounts were often read during meals, suitable both for entertaining with their wonders and for curbing immoderate appetites. Even the least learned monk had his head crammed with such stories.

The eremitic ideal, although never extinct, took on new vigor around the year AD 1000. At the turn of the eleventh century, St. Romuald rediscovered the joys of the "desert." Romuald came from high aristocracy, the Onesti dukes of Ravenna. Like his peers, he passed his youth in the violent pleasures of hunting and combat. However, one day, chasing prey in a forest, he found himself alone and longed for the contentment of the hermits of old who chose such retreats for their home. Then before his very eyes, Romuald's father killed an enemy in a duel. To expiate a crime for which he felt responsible, Romuald first went into a monastery. Soon he asked to be clothed in the monastic habit. Seeking perfection ever

---

of Nursia (ca. 480–ca. 547) is the author of the famous monastic rule that eventually became standard across medieval Europe (and was followed by the nuns of Fontevraud). Before founding the monastery of Monte Cassino in central Italy, for which he wrote his rule, Benedict had spent time as a hermit at Subiaco, not too far from Rome.

30. "Eremitic" means "concerning the life and practices of hermits."

further afield, he became a monk at Saint-Michel-de-Cuxa in Catalonia, far from his homeland. From Saint-Michel, he disappeared into solitude for three years. He ate nothing but chickpeas for a year, then fed himself only on Sundays, nourished by reading the *vitae* of the desert fathers and beset by demonic harassment. He returned to Italy and spread monastic life far and wide. In 1012, Romuald founded the monastery of Camaldoli in the heart of the Apennines, and on this settlement near Arezzo he imposed the rule he had dreamed of. The hermits of Camaldoli left their tiny cells only for prayer services and recluses of the community never went out at all. Silence and fasting were extreme: men did not speak at all during fasts and, except on Thursday and Sunday when they tried to satisfy hunger with vegetables, they subsisted on bread and water. Romuald's foundation accomplished his desire "to make the whole world a desert."[31]

Peter Damian, author of the *Life of Romuald*, was raised in this harsh life at the monastery of Fonte-Avellana, a replica of Camaldoli. In 1043, he became its prior. Peter's renown was such that he was continually appealed to amidst the conflicts that tore through Christendom in his time. Forced to accept a position as cardinal bishop in Rome under threat of excommunication, Peter dreamed of nothing but a return to Fonte-Avellana. The world, however, endlessly recalled him. He tirelessly defended the cause of ecclesiastical reform and was among those who paved the way for Pope Gregory VII. Whenever he could manage it, Peter Damian retreat-

---

31. Romuald (ca. 950–1027) modified the Benedictine Rule for hermits in the way described; his foundation was given papal sanction in 1072. See Peter Damian, *Vita beati Romualdi*, ed. Giovanni Tabacco (Rome, 1957), and, in an older edition, PL 144: 953–1008; partial translation by Henrietta Leyser in *Medieval Hagiography: An Anthology*, ed. Thomas F. Head (New York, 2000), 295–316. For a recent discussion of the Italian hermits who preceded Robert, see Cécile Caby, "Vies parallèles: ermites d'Italie et de la France de l'Ouest (Xe–XIIe siècle)," in Dalarun, ed., *Robert d'Arbrissel et la vie religieuse*, 11–24.

ed to his little cell and there, far from worldly honors, ate his daily bread from the dish that also served for washing the feet of the poor.[32]

It is sometimes said that the revival of eremitism was inspired by the revival of urban life in the West in the eleventh century and that this flight from the world was an escape from these nascent Babylons. This was surely true of Italy, at the beginning, but less evident in other places. The history of religious consciousness develops along its own lines. The link between the desertion of the world and the ecclesiastical reformers' ideal of perfection is permanence. In western France, the eremitic movement, somewhat late in it appearance, came in the wake of Gregorian initiatives and was contemporary with the preaching of the First Crusade. William Firmatus broke the trail in Maine, east of Brittany, and then came a blossoming with Vitalis of Savigny, Raoul de la Futaye, Bernard of Tiron, Hervey de la Trinité, Alleaume of Etival, and then to the south with Pierre de l'Etoile, Stephen of Muret, and Gerald of Sales.[33]

He who goes far from the world plays dice with his life: he can win everything or lose everything. To hell with the half-measures of ordinary existence! It will be the Devil or God, temptation before contemplation. The evangelical model of these retreats is the episode of Jesus' temptation in the desert. After forty days of fasting, Christ is tempted by the Devil three times but triumphs.[34]

---

32. Peter Damian (1001–1072), besides his activities as hermit and reformer, wrote an enormous amount of poetry and prose on religious subjects. Washing the feet of the poor was a common act of piety in the Middle Ages, done ceremonially by Benedictine monks on Maundy Thursday in remembrance of Jesus' washing the feet of His disciples before the Last Supper (see Jn 13).

33. This generation was active in the first third of the twelfth century. Like Robert of Arbrissel, a number of them ended up as sponsors of women's religious life. See Bruce L. Venarde, *Women's Monasticism and Medieval Society: Nunneries in France and England, 890–1215* (Ithaca, NY, 1997), 64–66, 164.

34. Lk 4:1–13.

Who, though, can lay claim to His power to prevail over the Prince of Darkness? The greatest hermits, Anthony and Romuald, sometimes called desperately for help against the Enemy's barbs. Therefore the warnings are equally classic. Benedict's Rule defines the conditions hermits must fulfill:

> There are those who no longer rely on a novice's fervor and who, by long service in the monastery, have learned to fight the Devil and are battle-hardened thanks to the support of their brothers. Then, well prepared, they go from fraternal warfare to single combat in the desert. Now, sturdy even without anyone's support, with God's help they are prepared to battle against the vices of the flesh and the mind with their own hands and arms.[35]

In two letters addressed to a hermit named Robert, who might be Robert of Arbrissel, the great Ivo of Chartres repeats these precautions and worries:[36]

> Take care, with the aid of divine goodness, that no foul spirit reaching toward you finds the house it has left empty inside and adorned on the outside, and that it does not bring along with it the seven other evil spirits disguised as virtues and thus make your new way of life worse than the old one.[37] That is why, to combat evil spirits, if you want to fight in certainty of victory, draw yourself up in battle order from the camp of the soldiers of Christ. For if you labor to fight in single combat,

35. This is from the first chapter of Benedict's Rule, which describes the different kinds of monks. For Latin text and translations of the Rule into several languages, see www.osb.org/rb.

36. Ivo (ca. 1040–1115), bishop of the west-central French city of Chartres for twenty-five years, was an expert in canon (Church) law who, in addition to legal collections and sermons, left an enormous number of letters concerning important matters of ecclesiastical politics in his time. The letters quoted below are edited and translated into French in Yves de Chartres, *Correspondance*, vol. 1, trans. Jean Leclercq (Paris, 1949), 138–141 (Letter 34) and 152–157 (Letter 37); Latin only in PL 162: 46, 49–50.

37. In Mt 12:43–45 and Lk 11:24–26, Jesus describes the unclean spirit returning to its first home and bringing seven more along with it, ruining the person whose soul they inhabit.

unprepared, against seasoned enemies, you will be crushed by an innumerable multitude of foes. But when you are in the habit of evading the traps of the Enemy, armed with the spirit of wisdom and strength and accustomed to spiritual combat, you will be able, should the occasion arise, to enter into battle on your own against all possible enemies whose assaults you have learned to bear in the line of fire. It is to this end that our Lord Jesus Christ warned His disciples who had not yet gained certainty in the Holy Spirit and training in spiritual warfare, saying, "As for you, stay in the city until you receive virtue from on high."[38]

A popular saying harshly sums up these eloquent discourses: "For a young hermit comes an old devil."

The desert is above all a spiritual space, a place of everything or nothing. The *eremum* of Robert and his companions was neither dry nor empty. That is not what matters; Baudri, who until this point had systematically specified the places his hero went, does not identify this new stopping place. It was a non-place. To hear Ivo of Chartres tell it, his correspondent, the hermit Robert, took refuge "on mountain rocks." There are no such summits on the map of western France. In Ivo's meaning they are simply the opposite of "this vale of tears," a symbol of the ascent of the soul toward God. People of this era saw the world, what we moderns call reality, through the prism of universals, of Platonic ideal forms.[39] The forested shallows that Western hermits loved were simply the pale reflections of the only thing that counted, the ideal; in truth, these

---

38. Lk 24:49.

39. In ancient and medieval philosophy, starting with Plato, is the notion that natural species, created objects, even substances and properties have a corresponding ideal in a world beyond human perception. In other words, a rose, a pitcher, or a shade of green visible here on earth is only a projection of an ideal American Beauty, Ewer, or Hunter—a "universal"—existing outside our realm. The view was controversial, and the subject of lively debate in the Middle Ages. Those opposed to the concept of universals, called nominalists, argued that the individual alone exists, and that universals are only human intellectual representations: ideas are only names (*nomina*), labels for a collection of similar things or ideas.

woods were the cliffs that overlook the Red Sea and the steps of Jacob's ladder.[40]

For us, that is either too much or too little. We like to place
things in space and time, as if that will hold for an instant a time
forever gone. So: in the spring of 1095, Robert of Arbrissel arrived
in the forest of Craon, on the border of Anjou and Brittany.

In the West, hermits' deserts were forested. An old Irish text
locates a green martyrdom of mortification and penance, green like
foliage, between the white martyrdom of simple renunciation of the
world and the red martyrdom of torture and death.[41] Made a "companion of wild beasts," Robert "inflicted himself with torture" and
"exhausted himself with cruel blows." His program was "to wear a
hairshirt of pigskin, to shave his beard without water, to know no
bed other than the ground, to refrain from wine and refined or rich
food, to sleep briefly, only rarely." It is almost disappointing. The
regime is austere, certainly, but not extreme, much less so than
the practices of those Egyptian champions, indeed barely harder
than the life of a peasant of the times. However, Baudri knew well
that this light asceticism, like Robert's delicate student clothes in
Angers, hid a more severe torture, an "internal conflict," a "roar of
the bowels," that pushed Robert to "conduct himself as an obstinate
and unjust enemy of his own self."

To others he was, to the contrary, "kind and restrained." This
desert was not only very green, but also quite populous. The medieval forest was never empty of people. It supplied a precious
abundance of resources: boar-hunters, anglers, lords' agents, and
woodcutters were all through it. Everybody went there for wood,

---

40. On Jacob's ladder, see Gn 28:10–22. The idea of a ladder reaching from
earth to heaven was a common theme in medieval writing.

41. The idea of the three martyrdoms, developed from the first days of Christianity in Ireland, is defined in a seventh-century Irish homily quoted in John Ryan,
Irish Monasticism: Origins and Early Development (London, 1931), 197–198.

for gleaning and gathering. Those who cleared land for cultivation nibbled away at its edges, slowly but surely. At the boundary of four provinces—Normandy, Brittany, Maine, and Anjou—the frontier forests of Mortainais, Avranchin, Fougères, Mayenne, and Craon were particularly popular at the end of the eleventh century. The so-called "solitaries" followed one another or met in the same places. Bernard of Tiron took up with William Firmatus at Fontaine-Géhard and at Savigny, which he later left, ceding the place to Vitalis and his disciples; this desert was too crowded for him. Usually there was no escape from company, but rather the opposite. The *Life of Vitalis of Savigny* bears witness to this network of hermits:

> Vitalis frequently received visitors including the most illustrious and honorable of his time—Lord Robert of Arbrissel, founder of the monastery of Fontevraud, Lord Bernard of Tiron, and other very famous hermits. Gathering at Dampierre according to the example of the ancient [Egyptian, ever and always] fathers, they discussed in frequent meetings the state of the holy Church and the salvation of souls.[42]

The extremely rich *Life of Bernard of Tiron* satisfies our curiosity even more: "On the boundaries of Maine and Brittany there were great solitudes that blossomed in these days like a second Egypt with a multitude of hermits living in dispersed cells." Under the guidance of Pierre de l'Etoile, Bernard, who had left a Benedictine monastery, went to ask admission to this desert. Vitalis of Savigny, one of the masters of this strange community, called a meeting of the hermits. Bernard was accepted into their number with enthusiasm, and each one offered his little cell to the new recruit. Bernard decided to visit all the cells scattered through the forest before choosing one. His decision took him to a cabin built in the ruins of an ancient chapel. Its inhabitant, Brother Peter, did not know how

---

42. Etienne de Fougères, *Vita B. Vitalis* [*Life of the Blessed Vitalis*], ed. E.-P. Sauvage, *Analecta Bollandiana* 1 (1882), 381.

to grow crops but lived by his skill with the lathe—which presupposes an economy of exchange. This turner-hermit, when chosen by Bernard, "danced with joy and taunted his fellows." Next, he improvised a meal:

> Quickly, he took up his baskets and went into the forest that surrounded his clearing on all sides. Without hesitation he tore through thorns and brambles and stripped hazel trees and others of their fruits. And when he had heaped up food of all sorts in his basket, he found in a tree's hollow a swarm of bees with wax and honey.

To this Peter added a pâté made with tree leaves. The hagiographer concludes, "This would have been a rich banquet had it not lacked bread, the noblest element of a feast."[43] Strange solitaries, strange ascetics! On the margins of established society, they lived a rural existence, a mixture of conviviality and independence. They were very free in these places where feudal society was most loosely stitched, and that was well worth not salting one's gruel of greens except on Sundays.

PREACHER

Aside from the company of his comrades, the hermit was also a man of encounters. His simple shelter was a haven for lost travelers. All of medieval literature testifies to this welcoming role. In the lands of the West at the end of the eleventh century, whole crowds raced toward hermits—to confer with them, to see them, to hear them. They played, then, the part of oracle. Their gift of insight allowed them to see the good or evil intentions of the questioner in a flash and to show the right path. A poor woman brought William Firmatus three eggs (eggs were a staple of the medieval diet, eaten in terrifying quantities); he said, "Daughter, take back

43. Geoffrey the Fat, *Life of Bernard*, sections 20–22 (Beck, *Saint Bernard de Tiron*, 336–339; PL 172: 1380–1382).

these gifts that you offer me wrongly, since they belong to neither of us." The woman insisted. "I have carved out of my poverty what I could to make a little offering to your holiness." Placed on the ground, the eggs turned into frogs. "Go," the saint told her, "and give back to your neighbor what belongs to him." When she did so, the eggs had happily returned to their original form.[44]

Some came simply to view these men of God. Their appearance, at once eccentric and conventional, drew attention: coarse, frayed, too short habits revealing knobby knees, plus unkempt hair and beards. Even better than to see them was to touch them, to share a bit in the gain of their asceticism. The hermit's body, all the more precious because it was willingly scorned, had a magical power. It suffered beyond measure; it contained the atonement of many and, consequently, their blessing. Nobody left the hermit as he had come. For this shift, this change, there was to be a reply, a countergift, like the little offerings pilgrims brought.

People went even more to *hear* Robert. His hagiographers were not the only ones to vaunt "his divine eloquence." Numerous charters extolled his thunderous voice and Abelard himself praised Robert's talent.[45] Robert was well aware of this gift, for which he thanked God on his deathbed. A few days earlier, the monks of the abbey of Déols, although quarreling with Fontevraud, had asked him to preach to them. More than just conveying a message, Robert was a virtuoso. People asked him for his art. A little later, we will examine one of his sermons that has survived. While there

44. Etienne de Fougères (?), *Vita S. Firmati* [*Life of Saint Firmatus*], section 17 (E.-A. Pigeon, *Vies des saints du diocèse de Coutances et Avranches*, 2 vols. [Avranches, 1892–1898], 2: 388–389 [French translation], 409 [Latin text]) and in *Acta sanctorum quotquot toto orbe coluntur*, 68 vols. (Antwerp, 1634; reprinted Brussels, 1965–1970; hereafter AASS), April, volume 3, 337.

45. Peter Abelard (1079–1142), a famous teacher and philosopher, praised Robert as "an outstanding herald of Christ" in one of his letters. See Venarde, *Robert of Arbrissel*, xv.

is no way to recall the charm of his voice and body, this was charm in a strong sense, an enchantment to which women were susceptible. In his first stages of preaching, Robert doubtless delivered a message as terrifying as his thunderous voice and as harsh as his homespun dress. He called for repentance and pulled no punches. An historian of the seventeenth century left us this testimony, unfortunately without revealing its source: "As often as he spoke, he instilled terror in the souls of sinners that those who did not keep God's commandments would fall into the depths of hell; those who hated him mocked him by calling him 'The Abyss of Hell.'"[46] Baudri rounds out the testimony: "He was known to rail against sinners in his sermons, but those who renounced sin he comforted with paternal affection." Many who approached struck their breasts on hearing him and decided to turn to good. They, in turn, underwent conversion. Such was the spiritual countergift that rewarded their journey—and "some of them came from far away."

Eremitism and preaching are, from one point of view, complementary. The personal asceticism of the hermit grants him the right to call others to repentance. In particular, the preacher accomplishes the mission of the seventy-two disciples mentioned in Luke's Gospel: "Take no purse, no bag, no sandals, and greet nobody along the way. . . . In every town where you enter and they welcome you, eat what is served you."[47] Robert, according to Brother Andreas, did exactly this, "always wearing a hairshirt and going barefoot to preach the Word of God, contenting himself only that listeners be given him to receive that which his nature had at last demanded [he give]."[48] From his first departure for the desert,

46. Jean-Baptiste Souchet, *Histoire du diocèse et de la ville de Chartres*, 4 vols. (Chartres, 1866–1873), 2: 362. The work of Souchet (1590–1634) was not published until the nineteenth century.

47. Lk 10:4, 8.

48. Andreas, *Second Life*, section 50 (Dalarun, *L'impossible saintété*, 289; Venarde, *Robert of Arbrissel*, 55).

he had taken care to bring along another priest. Here again is the literal adherence to the mission as set out in Luke's Gospel, since the disciples were to criss-cross the world in pairs. That sufficed for most saints departing for refuge or wandering, flanked by a companion. In the neighborhood of Craon, Robert reconciled for a while the two pursuits: "By day he strove to scatter the divine Word and by night retire to the desert to pray to God."

Eremitism and preaching are, from another perspective, irreconcilable. If some penitents returned home comforted and improved, others were unable to detach themselves from the master. "He would have fled such crowds of his own accord and hidden himself away all alone had he not feared to incur blame on that account." In fact, Robert knew that he could not push anyone away. So ended his time in the desert. To the day he died, he missed the solitude, the encounter with God. Encumbered by success, Robert had a duty to those who saw their salvation in him.

FOUNDER

They were his men. He was their master. His first duty, as he knew, was to feed them, like a lord has a duty to feed the men who have pledged faith to him. Feudal relations like these were so ingrained that even these marginal individuals, from their background of retreat, hastened to reconstruct them. Therefore, when Robert decided to found a religious community in the forest of Craon, it was, according to Baudri, for economic reasons above all. From the three eggs offered to William Firmatus to the offering of whole estates, the donation is one of the principal acts that cloaks an exchange in the Middle Ages. A religious foundation channeled, broadened, and regularized this flow of offerings. In exchange, Robert and his followers offered their intercession for benefits less tangible but highly prized. Thus the history of spirituality and economic history, far from being sealed off from one another, interpenetrate like barter. The lord Renaud of Craon made the first donation, that of the land of La Roë, where the community settled.

What status to give La Roë? At the end of the eleventh century, within the space of a few years, came a flowering of new or reformed religious orders. In 1084, St. Bruno founded La Chartreuse. For him there arose the same problem as for Robert, the need to reconcile eremitic solitude with the rules of cenobites, that is, monks living in community. In a place entrenched by the massif of Chartreuse, each monk cut himself off from the others in a tiny cell; the community was a juxtaposition of solitudes. In the order founded by Stephen of Muret, settled at Grandmont in 1124, the emphasis was on poverty.[49] In a supreme act of humility, the choir monks, literate and usually members of the ruling classes, were administered by *conversi*, lay brothers, rustics usually obliged to do the most menial work. Traditional monasticism, monks under Benedict's Rule, was not sheltered from this reforming breeze.[50] The splendors of Cluny did not at all match the aspiration to deprivation evident at this time.[51] In 1098, Robert of Molesme founded Cîteaux. In the first decades of the twelfth century, St. Bernard of Clairvaux would give considerable luster to the federation of Cîteaux, the Cistercians, a reformed branch of Benedictines. A great innovation in the Middle Ages was almost always a return to origins. In the case of Cistercian monasteries, the return to the Rule of Saint Benedict

49. La Chartreuse is in southeastern France, not far from Grenoble; Grandmont is in southwestern France, near Limoges.

50. There was no formal, structured "Benedictine Order" in Robert of Arbrissel's day. Most monasteries followed the Benedictine Rule, but were usually independent from one another. The novelty was in the new monastic federations mentioned here.

51. The monastery of Cluny in east central France was founded in 910 and soon became the head of a federation of dozens of monasteries. By 1100, it was renowned for its wealth and the splendor of its liturgical ceremonies.

in all its austerity was reflected in the impassive mirror of Cistercian architecture.[52]

This multiplication of foundations and reforms was unprecedented, its diversity a testimony to its importance. Everyone sought to respond in his own way to his calling. Thus it would be erroneous and unjust to reduce the "Gregorian" reform to the action of a single individual, the pope. All over Christendom, at all social levels, the same disquiet and the same hope worked on souls. One cannot but note the concurrence of this spiritual movement and the economic and demographic expansion that animated Europe in the eleventh century. A little more collective wealth (but also new inequalities), social tensions linked to growth, increasing mobility and exchange, a new inclination toward exploration and conquest—all these changes were related to the spontaneous reform movements, new aspirations, what Jacques Le Goff calls "another pioneer frontier . . . the frontier of the conscience."[53]

At La Roë, Robert founded an abbey of regular canons. Canons are not monks but priests. They follow the ancient Rule of Saint Augustine; one suspects that Robert advocated strict adherence to its call for asceticism, manual labor, and penury.[54] The choice of this rule is understandable in light of Robert's history. It was a means to reconcile the moral requirements of monks—chastity, poverty, and obedience—and the evangelism of secular priests fanning out to surrounding parishes. *Vita apostolica*, the apostolic life,

52. Cîteaux, like Cluny, is in Burgundy. Bernard of Clairvaux (1090–1153) was a famed preacher deeply involved in the highest levels of Church affairs in the first half of the twelfth century. Cistercians like Bernard distinguished themselves by careful adherence to the Rule of St. Benedict, and their churches were often built in a stark and unadorned style.

53. Jacques Le Goff, *Time, Work and Culture in the Middle Ages*, trans. Arthur Goldhammer (Chicago, 1980), 114.

54. The "Rule of St. Augustine" refers to one of several outlines of communal religious life written by the great North African bishop and theologian Augustine of Hippo (354–430).

was the label for this way of living that also referred to the tradition of the very oldest Christian community, that of the apostles.[55] Dividing their lives between the desert and preaching like Robert, the regular canons of La Roë simultaneously sought individual perfection and served others. In contrast to classic monasticism that acted only indirectly on the world through prayer, most of the new orders of the eleventh century sought to labor in the here and now, amidst humanity.

In February 1096, Robert received a ringing endorsement of his evangelism. Pope Urban II, who had just launched a call to crusade, passed through Angers.[56] Urban was curious to hear Robert, of whose reputation he had heard. Oddly and mistrustfully, the pope asked Robert to preach at the dedication of the church of Saint-Nicholas—and ordered him to refrain from unseemly remarks![57] Robert passed with flying colors and was invested with a fully official preaching mission and honored with the fine title of *Dei seminiverbum*, sower of the divine Word, God's chatterbox.[58]

Here was glory. Robert's sermons in neighboring dioceses drew such crowds to his side that, according to Baudri, La Roë would have been inundated if his hero had welcomed only a tenth of those who wanted to join.

55. See Acts 4:32–35.

56. Pope Urban II (1088–1099), once a monk at Cluny, toured the French lands in late 1095 and early 1096. In the south-central French town of Clermont, in November 1095, the pope first sounded the call for the European military intervention in the Eastern Mediterranean that we refer to as the Crusades.

57. Baudri's Latin describing the papal command is a double negative—*non insolitis mandat sermonibus uti*—that could mean "commanded him to use his customary discourse" as well as "commanded him not to utter strange remarks." Perhaps, by the use of such an ambiguous phrase, Baudri meant to suggest both the pope's desire to hear Robert and some uneasiness about this restless hermit's behavior on such an occasion.

58. *Seminiverb[i]us* is a rare word applied to St. Paul in Acts 17:18, the Vulgate Bible translation of the Greek *spermologus*, meaning "blabbermouth." On the history and medieval use of the word, see Venarde, *Robert of Arbrissel*, 120–121.

SEEKER

In a book that caused a stir in the 1950s, the East German historian Ernst Werner denied the authenticity of Robert's papal mission.[59] That the institutional Church remained cautious concerning this itinerant preacher is undeniable, but the historian from Leipzig, overly concerned to make his subject a defender of the oppressed against the powerful, misunderstood what connected the journey from humble priest of Arbrissel to consecration as *seminiverbum*. At the start was a loss of balance, the feeling of responsibility that grabbed Robert by the throat when he discovered that he was a sinner and the fruit of sin. This failure, he was taught, was the flesh. He despised it with all his might. He smothered it and shattered it, or so he thought. However, this same passion that set him against himself also pushed him toward others. He wanted to lead them to salvation. He failed as archpriest. He succeeded through the errant preaching of a penitent. Here he found charisma, the gift of God, in the omnipotence of the Word. The battle against simony and nicolaism, the call to repentance, the foundation of a house of canons—all went with the grain of the reform of the Church. It was natural that Urban II, his fears of excess allayed somewhat, rewarded such meritorious service, and that in particular he used this oratorical gift in the service of setting Christendom to rights.

The list of places furnishes other, more subtle indicators about the coherence of Robert's journey. One key theme in hagiography is the revelatory return to starting points. The beautiful story of St. Alexis, widely known around 1060 in its French version (the oldest literary text in the language) provides a perfect example.[60] Alexis, son of the noble Euphemian and Aglaia, grew up in Rome.

---

59. Werner, *Pauperes Christi*, 45.

60. "Life of St. Alexis," trans. Nancy Vine Durling in Head, ed., *Medieval Hagiography*, 317–340.

On his wedding day, desiring to preserve his virginity, he left for Edessa in Syria. There he gave away all his worldly goods and lived on alms under the doorway of a church. His desperate parents searched for him everywhere, but in vain. His exemplary life attracted too much attention, so after seventeen years Alexis returned to Rome and gained welcome at his father's house as a pilgrim. For another seventeen years he endured ill-treatment and insults from the servants there. In the end, his father had a revelation that the man who lived under his roof was one of God's saints. He raced to Alexis's side, only to see him die. In the pilgrim's hand was a parchment telling his story and his origin. Crazed with grief, his parents mourned their blindness. The anonymity of Alexis had earned him the highest recognition: sanctity.

Robert, through his ancestors, had deep roots in his corner of Brittany; he was a "native." When he had to leave his fatherland, it was as "an exile and fugitive." A journey to Paris was a trip to "France." Returning to his "home" diocese of Rennes was to come back on behalf of "his holy mother Church." Exiled anew in Angers, he left again, this time for Craon. Jean-Marc Bienvenu has rightly remarked that this part of Anjou was the closest to Brittany. Unable to return to the diocese of Rennes, where his zeal had made him too many enemies, Robert camped out on the frontier, within arm's reach of Arbrissel.[61] When Lord Hervey of L'Epine gave Robert's birth parish of Arbrissel to the abbey of La Roë, the circle was complete.[62] The prodigal son did not even have to return

61. Bienvenu, *L'étonnant fondateur de Fontevraud*, 28–29. It was only about twelve miles from Robert's retreat to his native village.

62. The cartulary of La Röe, that is, a collection of documents relating to its property made about 1190, is reproduced for viewing online at http://217.109.169.249/cg53v2/cartulaire.php. Documents relating to donations from Arbrissel begin on page 58 (that is, the back of the twenty-ninth folio). In the document recording Hervey's gift of the parish church of Arbrissel, Robert is called "a man of great authority and boundless faith who has sowed the Word of God in many places" and

to his land—it came to him. Robert of Arbrissel's story could easily end there.

---

the text notes that "many have gathered to take up the grain of such a sowing"
(*Roberto de Arbrisel viro magne auctoritatis et infinite religionis verbum Dei per diversa
loca inseminante, multi ad suscipienda grana tanti seminis convenere . . .*).

3

TRIAL BY FIRE

ROBERT ACCUSED

Yet he dreamed of nothing but escape. Devoting himself to a handful of canons meant neglecting the multitudes; sharing a stable life with these converts was to turn his back on lost sheep. Why preach to the converted? Baudri of Bourgueil, a little embarrassed, painstakingly recounts Robert's desertion, specifying that his hero did not act without the counsel of the bishop of Angers or the permission of his companions, and, at the base of it all, that Robert obeyed the command of Urban II that he preach far and wide.

He left, not without tears on both sides. In the few lines recounting Robert's hesitations and his departure from La Roë, Baudri oddly juxtaposes two themes: freedom and imitation. Robert decided "freely" to take to the road, to be "more free" to preach, and to go "without hindrance where he wanted, and with whom . . . without settling down in any one place." On the other hand, in choosing a life of wandering, Robert conformed closely to models. Going forth "without staff or pouch," he is much like the seventy-two disciples or, better still, the twelve apostles sent out to preach by their Master.[1] Like the Son of Man lacking "a place to lay His head," Robert performed the imitation of Christ.[2] There is no real

---

1. Lk 10:1–4. The quotations about Robert in this paragraph are from Baudri, *First Life*, sections 15–16 (PL 162: 1051–1052; Venarde, *Robert of Arbrissel*, 14–15).
2. Mt 8:20 and Lk 9:58.

contradiction between the two themes. The removal from La Roë was neither a show of disturbed instability nor the repetition of hagiographical clichés. Robert simply could not conceive of a freedom greater than to follow Christ step by step.

Disciples gathered immediately, an instant crowd, and Robert sought a place to establish them "without arousing scandal." With this discreet allusion, Baudri signals that it is not exactly the same story as before. This time, Robert was followed by disciples of both sexes. If there was a question of scandal, it was because of the women. Baudri says nothing more about it.

Marbode of Rennes makes up for the hagiographer's discretion in an epistolary indictment. Our attention now shifts to this document.[3] There is great temptation to create continuity across the discontinuity of sources, to find truth in a happy medium between contradictory opinions. However, this bland solution will not do. If Robert is to have a chance to be more than a silhouette, to have the depth that recalls the intensity of lived experience, it will be in an album of viewpoints that allows the play of what Pierre Toubert calls "the dialectic of testimonies."[4] It is Marbode's turn.

A contemptible outfit over skin chafed by a hairshirt, a cowl full of holes, legs half-naked, fuzzy beard, hair cut short at the brow—with this look you go barefoot into the crowd and offer an incredible spectacle to those present. They say you lack only a bauble to have the air of a madman.

It is always easy to jeer at the champions of the establishment. The insane—those of the past, at least—have our willing sympa-

---

3. Unless otherwise noted, discussion by Marbode summarized and quoted in this chapter is found in Johannes von Walter, *Die ersten Wanderprediger Frankreichs. Studien zur Geschichte des Mönchtums*, 2 vols. (Leipzig, 1903–1906), 1: 181–189, with a truncated version in PL 171: 1480–1486. Translation in Venarde, *Robert of Arbrissel*, 92–100.

4. Pierre Toubert, "Hérésies et réforme ecclésiastique en Italie au XIe et au XIIe siècles. A propos de deux études récentes," *Revue des études italiennes*, n.s. 8 (1961), 65.

thy. However, if we want to understand Robert of Arbrissel, we must listen very closely to the exhortation that Marbode of Rennes addressed to him between 1098 and 1100. First of all, the two men knew each other well. Marbode studied at the cathedral school in Angers, an institution run by the bishop's staff of canons, a center of intellectual revival. In time, Marbode became its director. He held this position for many years, guiding study in the diocese, reading and rereading the Christian authorities he cited as easily as he breathed, without neglecting the pagan authors he tried to equal with his poetry. He also addressed to his students a treatise on rhetorical figures. Hounded out of Rennes in 1093, Robert took refuge in Angers. Renewing his studies there, he put himself under the rule of a master some dozen years his senior. When Marbode was named bishop of Rennes, the two men doubtless traded words on the subject of his stormy election. Addressing Robert two or three years later in the longest of his surviving letters, Marbode simultaneously rebuked the preacher and blessed him as one of Christendom's men who mattered, which made him a target, one of those whose false moves put his entire following in danger.[5]

Marbode and Robert knew each other, acknowledged each other, and understood each other. Certainly their choices were different and nothing could less resemble the vagabond hermit's rags than the regalia of a bishop, full of the majesty of his responsibility. However, they were trained at the same school and spoke the same language. The wise man leads us to the madman.

Discretio is the keystone of Marbode's learned rhetorical edifice. It means judgment, wisdom, moderation, reason—we grope at

5. On Marbode's career, see Melissa Belleville Lurio, "An Educated Bishop in an Age of Reform: Marbode, Bishop of Rennes, 1096–1123" (Ph.D. thesis, Boston University, 2003). Lurio's careful study updates some of the standard chronology of Marbode's life; for example, he was probably not named master of the Angers school until at least 1075, although he was a strong learned presence there for some time before that date.

translation to explain an essential value of medieval Christianity. Robert lacked it on three counts. First, his appearance: not that the rags really surprised or shocked Marbode, for the good reason that they were hardly original. This was the uniform of a penitent, John the Baptist's. Evoking the second of Robert's faults, usurpation, his critic writes: "Your appearance is fitting neither to your profession, nor your wandering, nor your rags." Marbode recognizes the virtue of such a costume, the moral code it imposed on its wearers. But Robert, as canon and priest, had no right to it. He usurped a costume, and therefore a status, that was not his own. "For each profession, for every order there is suitable dress, which if changed offends public opinion." This was, after all, a society of orders, of castes, supported by thinking that reveled in classification: to the king his crown, the bishop his miter, the leper his badge, to the fool his bauble, to the lunatic fringe the appropriate costume.

To usurpation, Robert added excess. "Even in coarse and humble habit, we must preserve moderation handed down by the authority of common sense and tradition." Marbode develops at length the Aristotelian idea that virtue is a balance between two opposing vices. *Moderatio* and *mediocritas* are attained thanks to *discretio*. "Finery and filth should be avoided equally: the one smacks of pleasure, the other of pride." Here the bishop of Rennes does something more than preach the morality of the established order. In his ostentatious humility, does Robert not encourage people to talk about him, to increase his "prestige among the simple folk"? Proving that he is not so foolish as to think that the clothes make the man, Marbode adds, "What is praiseworthy is not to go around without linen dress, but to attach no value to linen." This call to interior piety, to subtle humility, would not have left Robert indifferent. In Angers, a few years earlier, he preferred to hide his hairshirt under a neat habit rather than complacently put it on display through holes in rags. Ten years later, we will see the same precepts coming from Robert's pen, nearly word for word. It would seem that in this case, Marbode's criticism carried weight.

It is perhaps surprising that a bishop shows such attention to sartorial matters. Marbode, though, was one of those for whom the right order of the world is in the details. Robert's outfit was but the introduction to other, more serious disturbances. "Furthermore, in the sermons by which you usually teach the common run of humanity, ignorant people, not only do you correct the faults of those present, as is fitting, but you enumerate, rip apart, tear to shreds the crimes of Church officials as well, which is not fitting."

Could there be a more blunt expression of class war than Robert, social agitator and defender of the poor, harassing the powerful? Marbode's letter crackles with this theme: its author does not hide his contempt for the masses, for the commoners that he depicts as ever fond of novelty and always ready to fall for a con man. The bishop states clearly that he speaks on behalf of a group of churchmen and laypeople tired of the vagabond's excesses. It is easy to imagine an assembly of these sober notables, disrupted from their ease and exasperated to see their privileges protested, deciding to take action by deputizing the bishop of Rennes to bring the troublemaker back to his senses.

Medieval guardians of high culture used language very carefully. Therefore it is necessary to examine closely the terms Marbode employs in order to avoid misinterpretation. Three times he uses *vulgus* or *vulgares* to designate Robert's followers, a "vulgar" we would readily translate as "the people." But Marbode had already used the term in a context that makes his meaning more precise: "Many people reproach you, not just ecclesiastics but also *vulgares personae*." Is the writer acting as spokesman for the masses? Evidently, these persons—these personages—identified in contrast to the clergy are laypeople, each side expounding "divine and human laws." Marbode's scorn for the crowds that follow Robert is that of a cleric for the laity, "ignorant people," or more exactly "non-experts," non-specialists in religion, who spoke not Latin but the vernacular language. The powerful people Robert attacked were members of the upper clergy. This was the "whole ecclesiastical order" Robert undermined in denigrating "dignitaries."

The bishop was clever, well versed in rhetorical tricks. If he asked Robert to choose between the powerful and the humble, would the hermit who wanted to be one of "Christ's poor" hesitate for a moment? In contrasting clergy with laity, Marbode was stirring up other solidarities, without doing so directly; by arguing slyly, Marbode succeeds brilliantly at attacking his enemy from the rear. Crimes committed by important people he does not deny, but he turns the situation into trouble for Robert. Isn't it just slander to criticize the absent? Who departs from such a denunciation morally improved? The powerful were appalled by the baseness of the act. The crowd would find itself authorized to act badly upon learning of the failings of its pastors, for "the quality of pastors is that whatever they do, they appear to show the way." Marbode is at his most stirring when he bemoans the fate of parish priests abandoned by their flocks in favor of the usurper Robert, "poor priests" thereby deprived of tithes that are legitimate payment for the care they take for the sheep that God has entrusted to them.[6] Marbode's is the art of turnabout; he makes Robert into a persecutor of the poor.

Thus it is not a question of conflict between the mighty and the humble, but one of ecclesiology. The debate bears on strategy for effecting Church reform. Were clergy unworthy? Marbode does not deny it. Should they be constrained to virtue? Undoubtedly. However, this was a matter of the internal affairs of the Church, not to be aired in the public square before laypeople well known to be untrained in matters of religion. Such is the lesson the schoolmas-

---

6. Tithes, literally "tenths," are the portion of goods or income that was to be given for the support of the Church.

ter gives his former student. It is undeniable that the question of social order is indirectly in play here. While defending poor priests'
tithes in a mournful tone, Marbode was protecting his own rev-
enues. By reaffirming the monopoly of the clergy in the sphere of
religion, he intended to reserve for his caste the power to manage
souls as they chose. Indeed, from each of his phrases there emerges
a certain vision of the universe, hierarchical and immutable: pastors
at the head of their flocks, parishioners at home in their parishes,
Robert at La Roë—everybody in his place, in the dress befitting his
status. So the world goes, as God wants it.

Robert of Arbrissel was not a defender of the poor in the sense
we would understand that expression today. Otherwise it would
make no sense that when his disciples emerge from anonymity, so
many are representatives of "the best families." Put precisely, his offense—there certainly was one—was not to choose the humble ex-
clusively, but to mix the sexes. "According to what reasoning is it
defensible that you indiscriminately receive men and women, of all
conditions and ages . . . ?" The mixing of sexes, classes, and generations is what Marbode finds truly unacceptable. A hierarchical society could not allow such leveling.

The year Robert died, a man of whom little is known, Henry of
Lausanne, traveled across the diocese of Le Mans followed by a
similarly mixed horde. Denouncing the unworthiness of clergy,
Henry advocated the right of all to priesthood and worship in city
squares and roads. Chased away from Le Mans, he disappears from
view for a while. His name surfaces twenty years later at a council
of bishops in Pisa, which condemned him. In 1145, the count of
Toulouse called in Bernard of Clairvaux to battle against him.
Henry was arrested, handed over to a papal legate, and incarcerat-
ed in a monastery. At that point his traces vanish for good.[7] In the

7. On Henry of Lausanne, see R. I. Moore, *The Origins of European Dissent*
(New York, 1977), 82–114 passim and 274–277.

limited view that hostile and incomplete sources allow us, Henry resembles the founder of Fontevraud in several ways. The paths of the two very nearly crossed and Robert almost incurred the same condemnation as Henry. A few years later, in a completely different set of circumstances, the Benedictine monk Guibert of Nogent trembled at the word "commune," the name for associations of citizens in the reviving cities of the day.[8] For Guibert, Marbode, and the enemies of Henry of Lausanne, the world was made and remained upright with a head and members, a vertical, pyramid-shaped universe that could not accept these horizontal solidarities among people. Moreover, look at them, these critics said: they wallow in themselves.

When Marbode considers Robert's disciples, exasperation gradually prevails over rhetorical skill. These followers, he writes, were inexperienced, welcomed into religious life without any preliminary consideration of their fitness, handed over to it by their own authority alone. They lived without discipline, for Robert immediately abandoned these converts, exposing them to damnation since he was interested in nothing but gaining more recruits. In view of the departure from La Roë, this criticism is not entirely without merit. It is the last arrow in Marbode's quiver. From here on, his finesse fails him and he foams at the mouth. In the end, what appalls him most is Robert's success: the number of disciples grows unceasingly and their bearing is despicable, a carbon copy of their leader's. "If you ask them who they are, they reply that they are 'the master's men,' without saying which one. . . ." They are hypocrites like Robert: they go barefoot in towns and villages, then put their shoes back on to travel across the countryside.

Finally, Marbode returns to the women in Robert's flock. He

---

8. Guibert of Nogent (1053–1124), monk and historian, is best remembered for an autobiography in which he recalls with horror the emergence of a commune in the northern French city of Laon.

began his diatribe on that point, and there he ends it. "By their appearance alone, they pour seductive poison into the marrow and rouse the dark places of the soul with insatiable lust." Robert's gravest failure of *discretio* was in his relations with the opposite sex. It is possible to guess at Robert's behavior based on Marbode's accusations, but the bishop of Rennes delivers more than that, including a reasoned moral lesson he commends to clerics and the frenzied images that haunt him.

Robert takes pleasure in cohabitation with women. At night, followers of both sexes stretch out in a jumble around him. Robert lies in the middle, arranging others' sleep and wakefulness. Female companions of his wanderings hang on his every word. He has settled other women in hospices and lodgings, in the service of travelers and the poor, foolishly mingled with men. The evidence is the wailing of newborns: some girls give birth in their little cells while others run away to hide their shame. Marbode does not, however, accuse Robert of having succumbed to sexual temptation. He knows this cohabitation is intended to atone for an old sin. He guesses at the wanderer's torment and cleverly wraps it in a blanket of innuendo. Robert errs in recklessness: is it reasonable to run right in front of the danger one is trying to avoid? What pride! Does he think himself holier than David or wiser than Solomon, who both fell into sexual sin?[9] Doubtless Robert's soul was not yet affected, but how firm did it stand? After all, he was not "of the impassive order of born eunuchs" but was instead one "of those who castrate themselves willingly for the kingdom of heaven," a race of

9. In 2 Sm 11–12, King David of Israel impregnates Bathsheba and then arranges to have her husband killed in battle, and God kills their firstborn in return for such wickedness. David's son Solomon, despite his wisdom, was turned away from exclusive worship of his god Yahweh in old age by some of his 700 wives; in return God saw to it that Solomon's kingdom was shattered after his death (1 Kg 11:1–13).

ascetics who are in great danger even far removed from women.[10] At the very least, Robert has the miser's perversity in amassing riches he does not intend to spend, even if his is not, in fact, the hypocrisy of a man passing for abstinent who feasts in secret on rich food and wine.

Beyond his condemnation of the hermit's lunatic asceticism, Marbode raises the question of priests in the world and their chastity. He does not manage to resolve it. He had been educated by the canons of Angers. Promoted to master of the cathedral school, he remained cloistered in this little clerical world. Now he was at Rennes amidst his cathedral chapter. Near the close of his life, he would resign from his prelacy to end his days at the monastery of Saint-Aubin in Angers. This secular cleric, who wrote hymns about chastity, wanted to live like a monk. Sympathetic to the reform of ecclesiastical morality, he nonetheless had great difficulty imagining a middle way between the canonical life, an attractive copy of cloistered monasticism, and concubinage, which he imagined as a stopgap: "To live in criminal continence and infamous holiness is worse than concubinage." In the end, Marbode cannot believe that one can avoid sin in the world, among women.

He cannot imagine chastity from afar, either. Like curls of smoke, women puff and swirl until they fill "the dark places of the soul." Marbode makes a fantastic storybook out of it. Woman is a temptress: "The origin of sin was the work of a woman and through her we all die." Woman is an enchantress: "Woman snatches man's precious soul. Take care lest your catch catches you!" Woman is a serpent, next to whom "it is not safe to sleep for long." Woman is a virus: "She spreads the plague of lust." Woman is a worm: "The moth comes out from clothing and the wickedness of men from woman." Woman is an itch and a poison that penetrates

10. In Mt 19:12, Jesus distinguishes between eunuchs from birth and those who have made themselves so for heaven's sake.

men "to the marrow." Woman is fire: "What will happen if the flame nears the straw?" Woman is a drunkard: "Why does one who does not drink wine enjoy the delight of wine?" Woman is a wine-skin and a womb: their wombs burst from their clandestine child-births like the old wineskins under the pressure of new wine.

Marbode's inventiveness is inexhaustible. While he addressed elegant poems to Countess Ermengarde of Brittany and Queen Matilda, extolling their beauty, he devoted part of his *Book of Ten Chapters* to "the prostitute," writing, "She has a lion's head, a ser-pent's tail, and everything in between is nothing but a burning fire."[11] Marbode vacillates between moderation and immoderation, cold reason and bursts of flame. Within Romanesque churches of Marbode's day, models of harmony and balance, a crowd of sirens, dragons, and vampires carved into the stone capitals sleep with one eye open.[12] In his poems, the censorious author confesses, "I was once tied down by the straps of insane love" and vows to the Virgin Mary that "what the body was not able to do, the spirit managed to carry through."[13] Like Robert, Marbode of Rennes was one of "those who castrate themselves willingly for the kingdom of heav-en" and who "with great effort can scarcely master this illicit ap-petite of the flesh, even in the absence of women."

11. Marbode wrote verse paeans to Countess Ermengarde of Brittany (ca. 1070–1147), the daughter of Count Fulk IV of Anjou, husband of Count Alan IV, and mother of Count Conan III (PL 171: 1659–1660) and to Mathilda of Flanders (ca. 1031–1083), daughter of Count Baldwin V of Flanders, wife of King William the Conqueror of England, and mother of Kings William Rufus and Henry I (PL 171: 1660). The *Book of Ten Chapters* is a work of Marbode's old age, a collection of long poems with deep philosophical, religious, and literary meaning (PL 171: 1693–1716). See also note 48 below.

12. On capitals atop columns in many cathedrals of the eleventh and twelfth centuries were elaborately carved tableaux featuring saints and marvels as well as wonders and grotesques.

13. The first of these lines begins Marbode's poem *Strictus eram loris* (PL 171: 1655); the second comes from *O sancta Virgo virginum (Nam corpus quod non potuit, mens perpetrare voluit),* (PL 171:1651).

Robert of Arbrissel never explained his own attitude toward women. His silence consigns us to conjecture, so much the more because his two biographers, quite understandably, avoid this delicate subject. Baudri gives only one hint, but a big one. Considering his wandering flock, about which he no longer knew what to do, the master had but one certainty, "that the women should live with the men." There was a purpose here about which Marbode of Rennes had not been mistaken. However, to understand Robert's idea, it is unjust to leave the last word, indeed the only one, to the prosecution.

What attracted Robert to women? To this question one can answer without fear of error that it was carnal desire. For the men of this era, woman and the flesh were but one idea; no male, whatever his status, could claim to escape a hunger that tormented the body or, worse yet, put the soul to the fire. This is the original impetus, the surging tide that the ascetic could not dam but only divert and channel in the service of his religious undertaking. On the basis of manly craving, Robert of Arbrissel designed a unique program.

Given the impossibility of knowing about it directly from Robert himself, we must try to understand it by analogy, to perceive it and hem it in with a network of examples and texts with similar concerns, models that the hermit certainly must have had in mind when his project took shape. Texts come first, because all certain knowledge rests in them, above all the *Lives of the Fathers*. At many centuries' distance, the excesses of these Egyptian solitaries constituted a great challenge to anyone who wanted to attain the kingdom of heaven by the narrow gate.[14]

St. Jerome recounted the life of Paul of Thebes. A legend rarely

14. Mt 7:14; Lk 13:24.

evolves in a straightforward manner—it detours often. The death of two anonymous martyrs opens this *Life of Paul.* Two young Christians were arrested by their torturers, who smeared the body of one with honey and exposed him to biting flies and wasps in the hot sunshine. He got off lightly. The other was put on the softest of beds in a dreamlike garden, amid the murmur of streams, the songs of birds, and the sweet fragrance of flowers. His captors tied down his hands and feet gently. Along came an exquisitely beautiful young girl who caressed him in a shameless fashion. Despite himself, he became aroused. He severed his tongue with his teeth and spat it in her face. Fondling by a woman was a form of torture, the most severe kind, one sweet to the body and thus placing the soul into extreme peril.[15]

In his *Conferences,* John Cassian recalled the undertakings of the most famous desert fathers. One of them, Paphnutius, thought himself free of all lust. Preparing a dish of lentils, he burned his hand in the flame and asked in grief, "Why can't fire keep peace with me, since I have won victory in far worse battles with demons?" An angel of God supplied the answer:

Why are you sad, Paphnutius, that this earthly fire will not leave you alone when there still lives in your body a seat of carnal tumult that has not been conquered? As long as its roots remain active in your marrow, they will not allow this material fire to be at peace with you. You will not cease to be sensitive to its attack until the day you prove by this sign that all interior fire is extinguished. Go and find a beautiful, naked young woman. If, upon touching her, you find that your body's tranquility remains undisturbed and the transports of the flesh are calmed, then, yes, contact with this visible flame will be sweet and harmless, as it was for the three children in the furnace of Babylon.[16]

15. Jerome, "Life of Paul of Thebes," in White, ed., *Early Christian Lives,* 76 (section 3).

16. John Cassian, *Conferences,* trans. Boniface Ramsey (New York, 1997), 543–545.

For the suffering martyr, contact with a woman becomes a voluntary torture and a kind of test. When a British ascetic, Kentigern of Glasgow, remained cold as marble after being plunged into icy water and then exposed to a very beautiful girl, he knew that his mortifications had not been in vain and that he had triumphed in the most arduous of battles.[17]

It is impossible to know if Robert of Arbrissel knew the Celtic tradition, so there is no need to dwell on it. The stories of the desert fathers suffice. At the same time, they were also inspiring Robert's close comrades, the forest hermits of western France. Some young troublemakers decided to mock William Firmatus and put his chastity to the test. They hired a courtesan who knocked at the holy man's door with a story that she was alone, feared wild animals during the night, and needed hospitality. The hermit immediately opened his hut, lit the fire, and gave her food. She pounced and he felt lust build. He picked up an iron from the hearth and applied it to his arm. Fire was vanquished by fire. The shameless woman fell on the earth and spoke her repentance.[18] For many years the scorched bone of this athlete of God was on view in the canons' church of Saint-Evroult in Mortain.

William preceded Robert by a few years in the western French wilderness.[19] Gerald of Sales was among his followers. During a preaching tour, a female troublemaker offered Gerald hospitality. He was warned by friends but paid no attention. Just as he fell asleep, she asked for her due. Gerald asked for a moment to prepare. He put his cloak over burning embers, stretched out, and in-

17. The bishop-saint Kentigern died in the early seventh century. The Gothic cathedral in Glasgow is dedicated to him.

18. Etienne de Fougères (?), *Vita S. Firmati*, section 8 in Pigeon, *Vies des saints*, 2: 381 [French translation], 401–402 [Latin text] and in AASS, April, volume 3, 335.

19. William Firmatus died in 1103 after many years as a hermit in western Maine, somewhat north of Robert's forest of Craon and La Roë.

vited her to join him and share his bed, if she liked. She, too, converted and took the veil at Fontevraud.[20]

All these ascetics were exposed to temptation and subject to *the* question, that of the flesh. This is "question" in the sense of "torture," but it was also a way to discover the truth. Those so challenged did not all reply in the same way. Prey to desire, some whipped themselves or flung themselves into nettles or thorns; they punished themselves and indeed as good as mutilated themselves. Others plunged into icy water or rolled in the snow. They healed themselves and become inured, treating fever with its opposite. Others fought fire with fire, the group we have just mentioned. They were the maddest. Robert was among them.

In feudal times, one of the regular forms of legal procedure was the Judgment of God, in particular the ordeal by fire and judicial duel. Whoever wanted to prove his innocence picked up a redhot metal object. If his palms resisted the fire, it was a sign that God wanted to proclaim his innocence.[21] In a dispute, the two adversaries or their designated champions faced each other. In granting one of them victory, God distinguished the guiltless from the felon. Dominque Iogna-Prat has quite rightly shown that in the penitential practices of western French hermits like William Firmatus and Gerald of Sales, and in the logic of John Cassian and Kentigern, testing by fire, a substitute for the flesh, had the value of an ordeal, of a test after a trial, an instant examination after long years of training in the desert. In this plea, God is asked to pronounce judgment, to give the contestant and his spectators a clear sign of guilt or innocence, of being prey to the Devil or close to sanctity, according to whether the body reacted to the burning or remained cold. Paphnutius was burned; he did not yet have full

20. Anonymous, *Vita B. Giraldi de Salis* [*Life of the Blessed Gerald of Sales*], in AASS, October, volume 10, 258–259.

21. See Robert Bartlett, *Trial by Fire and Water: The Medieval Judicial Ordeal* (New York, 1986).

control over his senses. William and Gerald could withstand the flame, a sign that carnal fire had been extinguished in them.[22]

Robert followed on and even distinguished himself in this ascetic tradition. Since his time in Paris, doubtless, the thought of his sin had gnawed away at him. Marbode guessed that this was so. At Angers and then in the desert he mortified the flesh so that his guilty body become like a corpse. There came a point when he asked himself, "Have I atoned enough? Have I overcome desire forever?" The test of the shared bed, the ordeal of the flesh, was designed to answer these questions. Robert substituted neither the heat of embers nor the scorching of red-hot iron for carnal fire. For William or Gerald, the challenge was met by overcoming an obstacle: whoever could withstand fire could withstand desire all the more. For his part, Robert took up the gauntlet, the call to judicial duel: he chose hand-to-hand combat.[23]

NEW SOLUTIONS, NEW ACCUSATIONS

The twelfth century arrived. Some years had passed since the vagabond had incurred Marbode's wrath when in 1106 another letter reached Robert. Its author was Geoffrey, abbot of the monastery of La Trinité in Vendôme and it, too, has survived. The correspondence of this era, even when it treated private matters, was not in any way confidential. Every letter was an open letter. The writer did not imagine one unique correspondent but the greatest number possible; he took care to keep a copy for himself so that the letter would survive him. Authorial self-consciousness? Not exact-

22. Dominique Iogna-Prat, "La femme dans la perspective pénitentielle des ermites du Bas-Maine (fin XIᵉ–début XIIᵉ siècle)," *Revue d'histoire de la spiritualité* 53 (1977): 47–64.

23. The original French here is "le corps-à-corps," literally "body to body," which better expresses Robert's struggle but does not correspond exactly to English idiom.

ly. Letter collections so constituted, far from being bits and pieces, had a meaning. They mirrored collections of legal decrees, built up like them piece by piece; these non-private letters were veritable summaries of jurisprudence. All the cases that Christian life brought to bear are examined in them and resolved with the citation of a multitude of authorities. Some authors covered so much material—like the canon lawyer Ivo of Chartres in 292 letters—that it seems their mail followed a prearranged plan. We have 186 letters by Geoffrey of Vendôme, divided into five books. In the forty-seventh letter of Book Four, "the humble servant of the monastery of Vendôme" addresses "Robert, his dear brother in Christ: may he observe the due measure of discretion and be content with the boundaries established by the Fathers of the Church."[24] If events had sometimes separated Marbode from Geoffrey—five years earlier, they had been on opposing sides of family quarrels over the election of the bishop of Angers—the two men still defended the same values, *discretio* chief among them, and they were similar in several ways. There was some of the monk in this bishop, and some of the bishop in this monk.

Geoffrey was born into the high nobility of Anjou, the family of the lords of Craon. He was placed in the monastery of La Trinité de Vendôme as a boy and in 1093 was chosen, very young, for the office of abbot. He left at once for Rome to receive the title of Cardinal of Saint Prisca, which was automatically awarded to the head of this powerful abbey. He insinuated himself into the good graces of Pope Urban II. He was a lifelong and tireless defender of the rights of the papacy, to the point that he did not hesitate to hurl

24. Latin text and French translation in Geoffrey of Vendôme, *Œuvres*, ed. Geneviève Giordanengo (Paris, 1996), 148–151 (Letter 79). The Latin text differs only very slightly from that in PL 157: 181–184 (Book 4, Letter 47). English translation in Venarde, *Robert of Arbrissel*, 103–105. Unless otherwise noted, Geoffrey's ideas discussed and quoted in the rest of this chapter come from this letter to Robert.

abuse at Pope Pascal II, who, in the abbot's opinion, had not defended papal prerogatives with sufficient conviction during the Investiture Contest. "Excuses? None admissible!"[25] Geoffrey was a formidable figure, touchy, haughty, and domineering. Called to a council at Orléans in 1126, he refused to accept the invitation from a papal legate because the abbot of Vendôme did not have to deal with anyone except the successor to St. Peter. When his monastery's interests were in jeopardy, his fervor knew no limits. Investitures performed by laymen and lay intervention in ecclesiastical or abbatial elections enraged him. He interfered with everything, especially matters that did not concern him, giving free rein to his affections and hatreds, never tolerating any challenge. Did someone oppose him? Then he wrote to Rome to obtain satisfaction. If necessary, he went there himself, apparently a dozen times. He triumphed and returned, more sure of himself than ever.

25. Geoffrey of Vendôme, *Œuvres*, 272–281 (Letter 134); PL 157: 42–46 (Book 1, Letter 7). The most specific criticisms, including the toleration of excuses, are toward the end of the letter. The Investiture Contest is shorthand for a protracted struggle between popes and the German emperors. Its overriding question was who was to have ultimate authority in Christendom: popes or emperors. "Investiture," strictly speaking, is the granting of the ring and staff to a newly elected bishop or abbot, long the prerogative of secular rulers, in many cases performed after choosing the new official themselves. This traditional practice came under attack in the middle of the eleventh century, but, starting in 1075, Pope Gregory VII insisted on enforcing a prohibition on lay investiture, that is, the installation of new bishops and abbots by lay people. The person he had most in mind was the German emperor Henry IV, who refused to acknowledge the ban and was subsequently excommunicated. So began a fifty-year struggle between six successive popes and Henry IV and his son and successor Henry V, amidst frequent warfare in Germany and Italy. Resolution came not until 1122 with the Concordat of Worms. The legalistic solution was that prelates were to be freely elected and consecrated by other ecclesiastical officials, but that secular lords were permitted to be present at the election and also to invest new bishops and abbots with a scepter symbolizing the property attached to the office. The idea, then, was that secular investiture by secular lords was permitted, but spiritual investiture or consecration was the purview of the Church.

Given his temperament, the measured and even affectionate tone of the letter addressed to Robert is all the more notable. Geoffrey begs "holy prayers" from his "beloved brother." Yes, there is once again a question of "sinister reports," and yes, once again the danger arises from women. However much Marbode's letter recalls the smacking of knuckles with a ruler, Geoffrey's betrays a real deference toward his addressee. "You have climbed a high mountain in this world and thereby turned people's eyes and tongues toward you."

In the interval between the compositions of the two letters, the status of Robert and his company had indeed changed. Was this the consequence of Marbode's criticism? Had it been ordered at the Council of Poitiers by papal legates?[26] Was it another instance of the process apparent in the founding of La Roë, a sort of natural evolution that causes a new swarm of bees to one day settle in a hive? In any case, in about 1101, Robert and his disciples fixed their sights on "a rough and neglected place, full of thorns and brambles"—Fontevraud.[27] Life, mirroring the place, was harsh and barracks-like. This "army of God" established an isolated camp, a desert. Miserable little huts barely protected them from the weather and they had only a simple oratory for prayer to God. Everyone was assigned a task to ward off idleness. All were to keep discipline, "neck bowed and face down," in silence; humility was the watchword. The troops took the fine name of *Pauperes Christi*, "Christ's Poor." Their leader, rejecting the title of abbot or lord, wanted only to be called their master. Fraternity reigned among them, with "no bitterness, no jealousy, no strife." It was a golden age.

26. Robert, along with fellow hermits Pierre de l'Etoile and Bernard of Tiron, had been among those at a council of Church officials held at Poitiers late in the year 1100.

27. The account and quotations in the next few paragraphs come from Baudri's *vita*, chapters 16–20 (PL 162: 1051–1054, translated in Venarde, *Robert of Arbrissel*, 14–18).

Monastic orders are nostalgic about their beginnings. In destitution, sharing, and concord, each new foundation revived for a time the early Church, a brief period when life, harsh but streamlined, seemed singularly easy. The little valley near the Loire did not reach the summits of La Chartreuse. In choosing Fontevraud, Robert at last demonstrated moderation and good sense. The place was not really a wilderness. Rather than deep woods, Baudri specifies, it was "a little forest, a thicket." In fact, Candes and Montsoreau were close to this desert, which was bordered by vineyards and where there were already two mills.[28] This was a good place, practically and politically. Robert found himself happily placed on the boundaries of principalities and dioceses. At the edge of the dioceses of Angers and Tours, Fontevraud was subject to the diocese of Poitiers, of which it constituted the extreme northern fringe. Thereby escaping the influence of the incompetent and the corrupt, the community found itself under the protection of Peter II, the pious bishop of Poitiers, who was to grant it much favor. But with this fortunate situation also came a danger. The Poitevin lands were subject to William, also the duke of Aquitaine, the very man who would years later have Peter killed through ill-treatment. On the other hand, the foundation itself was in the territory of the lords of Montsoreau and therefore in the orbit of the count of Anjou, so there was nothing to complain about there. For the moment, Gautier of Montsoreau and his kin granted the property to the new community.

At last, Robert mingled the sexes in good order. If it mattered to him that men and women live together, then it had to be done without scandal. So he put them in two separate places. Women,

---

28. Candes and Montsoreau were on the Loire itself, only about two miles north of Fontevraud. The charters granting the land to Robert and his followers mention a public road in addition to the two mills, one of which was apparently donated to the new community (PL 162: 1104).

consigned to the cloister, devoted themselves to prayer, while the stronger sex was compelled to the active life. There were subtleties: priests sang psalms and celebrated mass, while the troop's lay people, as Baudri says, "voluntarily submitted to labor." Here was a reintroduction of categories dear to Marbode, including unreserved recognition of priestly functions.

Fontevraud was a stunning success. "Nearly numberless" new recruits flocked there, especially women of all sorts and conditions. Feeding the crowd was a problem. Amidst unfarmed thickets, the new arrivals had not yet had time to clear, work, plant, and harvest. The hard work by which armies of land-clearers, never so active as in this era, remade the European landscape, was still in process. Fortunately, food came from the neighborhood, especially bread, the absolute essential. However, the army of God was too large and did not have something to eat every day. Robert made a sortie and spoke. His powers of persuasion were great enough to suffice. Offerings doubled. After bread came more food, clothing, and money. The gifts did not come only from local lands. Princes and common people came to see this odd congregation, "weak and pale under its thrifty regime." Before a year had passed, so much money had been gathered that yesterday's poor people, increased by the next day's recruits, were able to replace their huts with stone shelters and expand the oratory. These permanent constructions permitted the reinforcement of compartmentalization, making it more watertight. The men were put in housing out of the way and the women in turn were separated into two groups; the main group of them, over 300 strong, were placed in the major cloister.[29]

The firm but respectful tone of Abbot Geoffrey's letter must be understood in relation to this evolution. If Robert refused the ecclesiastical title of "Abbot" and the feudal power of a lord, a *domi-*

---

29. The men's community, dedicated to St. John the Evangelist, was some 200 meters from the women's compound.

nus, then he assumed the title of "Master." In Baudri's view, this mastery was, according to the spiritual authority it implied, nothing but the most perfect expression of humility; Marbode had bristled at such a total submission by the "master's men." Most of all, instead of going about with a bunch of faddish fools in train, Robert now ruled over a duly constituted ecclesiastical community, with the clerical and lay sponsorship necessary for recognition in this society of dominance and subordination. Even the master's appearance had changed, as Baudri bears witness:

For a long time, Robert had no horse and tasted neither wine nor seasoned food. He always went about barefoot and wore tunics and sackcloth. He continued these practices until one day, on the advice of priests, he put on shoes, got on a horse, and was for a little while milder with his tired body—not for pleasure, but to have more strength for his work.

The priests had applied pressure and brought the vagabond back to the right path. Robert settled down; he sat.

Geoffrey's criticisms are quite discreet. He makes no allusion to the dress of either Robert or his followers, nor is there any trace of group beddings-down in the woods. The two sexes were apparently by this time well separated, each in its own fortress. For men, the temptation was reduced to knowing that the women were nearby, sheltered behind walls. The scenery had changed, too. Murmurs in corridors and sounds from alcoves replaced the rustling of trees.

Five or six years after the foundation of Fontevraud, he alone had not renounced these peculiar scourgings, by then turning them into the master's privilege. Geoffrey wrote: "Word is that you permit certain women to live intimately, that you very often speak with them in private, and that frequently you do not blush to sleep among them at night." Robert liked it in the forbidden quarters. "In this way, so you claim, you believe that you worthily bear the cross of Our Lord and Savior by trying hard to extinguish carnal ardor wickedly aroused." This detail is extremely precious, because it appears to describe Robert's idea. The alchemy of his asceticism is to transmute the passions of the flesh into to the Passion of Christ. Geoffrey summarizes the practice in one word: sacrilege. "You crucify yourself in their bed with a new kind of martyrdom."

Twice the abbot stresses the novelty of this torture. "You have discovered a new and unheard of but fruitless martyrdom. Something contrary to reason cannot bear any fruit nor have any use." Geoffrey was mistaken in attributing the invention of this behavior to his addressee. As we have seen, Robert only perpetuated a deep-rooted tradition. The critic knew that perfectly well, since he immediately understood the practice as a martyrdom and crucifixion. However, "tradition" was already too vast and too diffuse to allow extravagant uses of it. It is notable that here at the dawn of the twelfth century, Geoffrey was trying to abstract from tradition whatever conformed to moderation and logic, at the same time that Anselm of Canterbury offered "faith seeking understanding."[30] To restore reason, there is nothing like a dose of Ecclesiasticus: "Do not lie down with a woman, nor be too solicitous of her; do not look at her lest you are enticed by her beauty and perish"; "Woman snatches precious souls"; and "Her conversation sets fire to man's heart."[31]

Unlike Marbode, Geoffrey does not insist too much on the point. The abbot's reproaches are not exactly about that. He addresses the leader rather than the ascetic. "Indeed, I have heard tell that toward the female sex that you have undertaken to guide, you follow two modes of conduct contrary to each other, but both ex-

---

30. Anselm of Canterbury (ca. 1033–1109) was a Benedictine monk and abbot, elected archbishop of England's most important diocese in 1092 and a major figure in the history of Christian thought. He was in the vanguard of an approach to faith as understood by reason and dialectic rather than citation of Scripture; his proof for the existence of God has been influential since its first appearance.

31. Sir 9:3–9; Prv 6:26. Geoffrey quotes these three sentiments in his letter.

ceeding the bounds of *discretio.*" In the eyes of his contemporaries, Robert specialized in the governance of women, "a hard task that has very often led those who have undertaken it to their deaths," Geoffrey warns. Of these two modes of conduct, we already know one: excessive familiarity and a shared bed. "As for the others, if you ever speak to them, it is with excessive strictness and pitiless harshness; you actually torment them with hunger, thirst, and nakedness and you never show them any compassion."

Much ink has been spilled over these phrases. The description, precise as to the contrasting treatments, is vague about the women who submitted to them. This imprecision has allowed very divergent interpretations to develop. For the time being, it must be admitted that despite all this discussion of women, they remained an anonymous mass. This is not our doing. The two letters addressed to Robert offer no details about the female battalions of which they make so much, and the abbot of La Trinité poses a question that he gives no means to answer. All the sources gathered together hardly suffice. Who were these women?

ROBERT'S WOMEN

To begin with, what was their social class? The internal organization of Fontevraud appears to provide clues. When Robert died, there were four different establishments in the abbey's complex: Saint John for men, Saint Lazarus for lepers, and two cloisters for women, the Great Monastery dedicated to the Virgin and the Magdalene.[32] For whom were these two women's houses intended? Certainly great ladies of the aristocracy came to take refuge at Robert's side and young girls were entrusted to him. Furthermore it is known that he drew fallen women to him. One idea is that the two cloisters welcomed women from these two ends of the social

32. See Prigent, "Fontevraud au début du XIIᵉ siècle," 276, for a map.

spectrum: repentants went to the Magdalene, virgins and well-born widows to the Great Monastery. On this basis historians like Jules de Pétigny found that Geoffrey of Vendôme's letter condemned the cruelties inflicted on the prostitutes by their master. Others, like Jean-Marc Bienvenu, came to the opposite conclusion: that Robert cherished the repentants and was harsh with the women of great families.[33] Both interpretations confirm a dichotomy. Is it actually visible in those few cases where a glimpse is possible?

Doubtless there were prostitutes in Robert's following. Baudri tells us that among his followers were *meretrices*, an ambiguous term that could refer to whores or, in a moral sense, loose women. However, another text, in which Robert enters a brothel and leaves with its residents headed for the desert, removes all doubt.[34] It is equally certain that there were titled noblewomen among Robert's recruits. They are the only ones whose names we know and whose stories we can more or less piece together. They warrant notice here.

Two women emerge from the troop of disciples by the eminence of positions they held: Hersende and Petronilla. Their Christian names appear in the two *vitae*, linked to Fontevraud. Once the construction of permanent buildings began, Robert returned to the road. As when he left La Roë, he departed to preach far and wide, to win new souls. He entrusted Hersende with care of the novice community. From the beginning, reports Baudri, she had followed Robert into religion, scorning her considerable nobility. Petronilla joined Hersende. When Robert wanted to put an abbess at the head of his order, the death of Hersende limited his choice to Petronilla. Andreas, the second hagiographer, reports at length all the stages of her election. Before an assembly of clergy he had summoned,

---

33. Jules de Pétigny, "Robert d'Arbrissel et Geoffroi de Vendôme," *Bibliothèque de l'Ecole des Chartes* 15 (1854), 9–11, 17–18; Bienvenu, *L'étonnant fondateur de Fontevraud*, 91.

34. See chapter 4 below.

Robert argued that rather than confer leadership on a virgin raised in the cloister, little experienced in practical affairs, he preferred to give it to a *conversa laica*, a female supervisor who had lived in the world, capable of managing material concerns. An archdeacon encouraged the idea: he had heard that Urban II had not hesitated to name as abbess a woman who had had four husbands. Shortly thereafter, the order was placed under the authority of Lady Petronilla—widow of the lord of Chemillé, historians add.[35]

Hersende and Petronilla can be identified by sources other than the two *vitae* of Robert, in particular charters that mention their names and that have allowed genealogists since the seventeenth century to locate them in the aristocratic lineages of the region. They were well-placed ladies. Hersende was the daughter of Humbert I of Champagne. Her second marriage was to William, the lord of Montsoreau; she was his third wife. She was thus the stepmother of Gautier of Montsoreau, the protector of Fontevraud; and since the latter held the lordship on the banks of the Loire when Fontevraud was founded, it must have been the case that his father was already dead and Hersende a widow.

Petronilla was a daughter of the house of Craon and therefore a first cousin of Geoffrey of Vendôme. Married to Orri the Red, lord of Chemillé, as the genealogists assert, she had at least two sons by him. When she met Robert, she was very young, perhaps less than twenty. When did Orri the Red die? Nobody knows. So was he already dead when she joined Robert's community? Whence the idea that Petronilla was a widow? In dedicating his *vita* of Robert to the abbess, Baudri makes no mention of widowhood. Nor does Andreas, who recounts her election. Yet it is through this second account that the idea slipped in. In the sixteenth century, there appeared two French versions of Andreas's *vita*. Under the pen of the trans-

---

35. Andreas, *Second Life*, chapters 5–7 (PL 162: 1059–1061; Venarde, *Robert of Arbrissel*, 28–30).

lators, the *matrona* promoted to abbess by Urban II despite her four marriages became a "veufve," a widow, even though for the moment Petronilla remained a "lay convert." In seventeenth-century historians' accounts of the Order of Fontevraud, widowhood became contagious and Petronilla was infected. From that point, despite the Latin *vitae*, this "fact" was systematically repeated by all concerned.

This thread of confusion shows the distance that separates us from the medieval period and our difficulty in acknowledging its peculiarity. If an abbess is not a virgin, then she must be a widow: since early modern times, no other scenario had been imaginable because it would appear unbecoming the dignity of the office—and if the sources do not say it, then we must make them do so. What do the sources really say? Petronilla is called a *conversa laica*, a "lay convert," because she renounced the world in which she had lived before and in which she had known the marriage bed. When she came to Robert's side, though, she left not her husband's house but her father's. Had she retreated there as a widow, a repudiated wife, or in flight from her husband? On this point the sources are careful not to be decisive. Petronilla's case is not clear and therefore interesting, since it has the purpose of drawing attention to the marital status of the women who converged on Fontevraud. The few other cases about which we have some information confirm that this status was quite problematic by our contemporary norms.

Ermengarde was the daughter of Count Fulk IV of Anjou. Perhaps she had been married to William IX, count of Poitou and duke of Aquitaine, who had disowned her. Certainly she married Alan Fergent, the count of Brittany. In 1112, her husband retired to the abbey of Redon and perhaps she used the opportunity to take the veil, a situation that was completely legal, anticipated, even encouraged by the Church. However, six years earlier, fleeing Count Alan and the primitiveness of Brittany, she had already taken refuge at Fontevraud after having tried in vain to have her marriage dissolved on the pretext of consanguinity. The retreat was temporary;

Ermengarde returned to the court of her son, Alan's successor, while her husband remained in the cloister until his death.

Agnes was the prioress of Orsan, a daughter house of Fontevraud and where Robert died. She was the countess of Aix-en-Berri and the former wife of Alard, lord of Châteaumeillant. Their marriage had been dissolved by reason of consanguinity and Alard had married again to a widow of the Bourbon clan. Agnes took refuge with Robert. What interplay of alliances and interests did this divorce hide? Which partner wanted to leave the other more? Was it the product of a quarrel, mutual consent, or payment? The only certainty is that Alard established his wife's priory through his own gift.

Philippa was the second wife of William of Poitou, perhaps succeeding Ermengarde in this formidable position. She was certainly under her husband's authority when she took refuge at Fontevraud in 1116, weary of William's infidelities and his notorious affair with Maubergeonne.[36]

Bertrade of Montfort married the count of Anjou, Fulk IV, making her his fifth wife and Ermengarde's stepmother. Then King Philip I of France took his vassal's wife. The Capetian king was dogged by the wrath of the Church and excommunicated several times. In 1105, the lovers promised to part. Only death accomplished the separation when Philip expired in 1108. Bertrade dreamed of an untaxing withdrawal from the world, but she acted deliberately. From 1108 to 1114, she paid at least four visits to Robert before deciding to shut herself away in the priory of Hautes-Bruyères, a daughter house of Fontevraud. She died there soon after.[37]

Peter the Venerable, abbot of Cluny, recalled the case of his

---

36. On the matter of consanguinity in general and William IX's marital history in particular, see chapter 2 above.

37. The case of Bertrade, Fulk, and Philip is a centerpiece of Duby, *The Knight, the Lady, and the Priest*; see especially 3–18.

mother, St. Raingardis. She could not endure marriage, hating its ties and, doubtless, her husband. When she heard casual mention of any holy man, she hastened to throw herself at his feet and ask him to take her under his protection. It was the same for Robert. He calmed her down and advised that she wait for the death of her lord and master. (Such caution was unusual. A letter from Roscelin to Peter Abelard states that Bishop Renaud de Martigné of Angers took Robert to task because when husbands clamored for their wives who had taken refuge with him, he turned a deaf ear.) What matters here, though, is Raingardis's attitude: "She threw herself at holy men's knees and, like Mary the sinner, she watered their feet with tears." If Robert had welcomed this woman, would he not have put her in the Magdalene, rather than the Great Monastery, since Raingardis's own son did not hesitate to compare her to Mary the sinner, whom we call Mary Magdalene?[38]

Along with peaceful widows and shy virgins, wives rejected by husbands or in flight from them crowded Fontevraud, women eager to share intimacy with the fascinating founder. Others, conversely, little inclined to give up the pleasures of the world, entered the cloister with regret, near death, only to ensure their imperiled salvation. The distinction between noble ladies and prostitutes ultimately proves unworkable. To a cleric, Bertrade was a *meretrix*, whatever her rank. To her own son, Raingardis was a Magdalene. Close examination of these few individual cases—that is, those one can decipher, concerning members of the ruling classes— encourages rejection of a clear bipolarity, an extreme opposition among the female recruits who were Robert's disciples. In the troop that followed Robert before he settled at Fontevraud, we

---

38. *The Letters of Peter the Venerable*, ed. Giles Constable, 2 vols. (Cambridge, MA, 1967), 1: 158–159 (part of a long, pseudo-hagiographical account of Raingardis in Letter 53). For the letter by Roscelin, a Paris schoolmaster who was a rough contemporary of Robert of Arbrissel, see PL 178: 361 and François Picavet, *Roscelin: Philosophe et théologien* (Paris, 1911), 132.

should imagine, besides virgins, an infinite diversity of cases, a spectrum ranging from a few "irreproachable" widows to a few professional prostitutes.

These women all had one thing in common: they were the victims of the matrimonial crisis that rocked Christendom at that time, a crisis that Georges Duby has unveiled.[39] Since the beginning of the eleventh century, the Church had waged war on all fronts. Not content with the attempt to impose celibacy on its clergy who lived in the world, it wanted to moralize the couplings of lay people—that is, to impose its morality in the form of marriage consecrated by the Church, unique and permanent, whose partners had no blood kinship or at least only a distant one. It was, in short, the model of marriage that for better or worse has survived to our times. This clerical morality, as the representatives of the Church presented it, was not the rationalization of chaos but an alternative to an old order of marriage, a different code. Among the powerful, where we can see the workings of this old order, marriage obeyed the dictates of lineage: assurance of heirs and increase of property. A husband dismissed a wife who did not provide him with sons. If a more advantageous match presented itself, he preferred new hopes to the existing union. To avoid dispersing the family patrimony, he willingly married his cousin. To show his prowess and virility, and to keep his rank, he kept beside him women of lesser grade, "Danish wives," as the expression was at that time. In the absence of an heir of better bloodline, the sons of these unions might inherit, although not without difficulty since their rights were not as clear as those of children born of spouses of the first rank: witness the trouble William the Bastard had in becoming the duke of Normandy.[40]

---

39. The paragraphs that follow derive in large part from the conclusions of Duby, *The Knight, the Lady, and the Priest.*

40. William (ca. 1028–1087) was the son of Duke Robert by the daughter of a tanner. His father named him as successor when William was a boy, but kinsmen, other powerful Normans, and men from outside Normandy resisted the unusual

These two models of marriage differentiated by Georges Duby came into conflict around 1100, just when Fontevraud was established. The "abduction" of Bertrade of Anjou by King Philip I and the conflicts that followed were centerpieces in the debate. Little by little, the priests imposed their law and, first of all, their words: "incestuous" for those who married despite close kinship; "adulterer" or "bigamist" for a man who took a new wife after dismissing a sterile spouse or one of less exalted rank; "concubine" for any woman accepted into a man's bed whose rights the Church did not recognize; "*meretrix*" for a woman of lesser status who shared a master's bed when he desired. The knights, faced with this assault on their traditional prerogatives, first stiffened their resolve, then used cunning, discovering consanguinity with wives of whom they wanted to be rid, turning the clerical message back against itself. Finally they submitted. The contagious widowhood of Petronilla of Chemillé shows how completely the Church triumphed. After the Middle Ages, it was unimaginable that there ever could have existed another legitimate order besides the one advocated by the clergy.

These two moral models, that of the warriors and that of the priests, conform on one point. Both belong to males. In their conflict, the woman is nothing but a manhandled object. Robert opened his arms to women condemned, rejected, or fugitive. The onetime nicolaite priest, pursuing his project of mad asceticism, and the distraught wives met on common ground. The success of Fontevraud is the fruit of this necessary risk, this apparently preposterous association of the victims of new moralities. For victims they were, on all counts. First, there were the victims of the warriors' codes, of marriage as princes, barons, or knights conceived of it, rejects, sent away on account of barrenness or abandoned for

---

step of making an illegitimate child heir to a great duchy. Later William successfully invaded England, to the throne of which he had a dynastic claim, and is best known to history as William the Conqueror.

better alliances—like Agnes of Orsan, whose husband suddenly discovered they were cousins, sheltering behind the language of the clergy to attain his ends. There were also those women who awoke to other aspirations and fled husbands too brutal, crude, or faithless. Like Ermengarde and Raingardis, they thirsted for mysticism and were ablaze for the fascinating apostle and did not know how to rid themselves of their husbands, or, like Philippa with the duke of Aquitaine, they could not endure their infidelity. Like Petronilla, they nursed ambitions beyond escaping from the control of their fathers only to fall under that of their husbands and back again. Secondly—cases less visible since they mostly concerned the less aristocratic—some of the women fell victim to the new battle joined by the Church. They suddenly found themselves immoral, "incestuous" or "concubines" by virtue of those ties that had until then appeared perfectly natural. This was the story for Agnes and Bertrade, but also for how many wives of lower rank, priests' wives touched by Gregorian commands, pregnant servant girls, loose women, packed off for Fontevraud to hide a now illegitimate status? To Fontevraud, doubtless, flocked those young girls who, according to Marbode, gave birth in their cells or, worse still, fled Robert's band in turn to have a baby in the woods, overtaken by panic and new shame.

In the times of wandering and the beginnings of Fontevraud, women went along every which way, joined with men, and interacted among themselves without regard to birth and rank, much to the dismay of Marbode and his friends. Then came a time—possibly the result of criticism and pressure—when Robert gave himself up to classification, separated the sexes, and divided the troop of women, apparently into two groups, since two different houses welcomed them. This division, as already noted, is problematic. Only a very close reading of Robert's *vita* yields the key to understanding. On his deathbed, Robert called Fontevraud to mind: there were his priests and clerics, there too his holy virgins, widows, and chaste women.[41] These three female groups divide into two categories: virgins and others. These were moral categories, as Robert wanted them to be, those who had never approached men and those who had known them. It was between the two categories of cloister virgins and lay converts that Robert deliberated before choosing an abbess. The first group, recluses in the Great Monastery vowed to the Virgin par excellence, grew ever richer, their numbers increased with well-born daughters offered to Fontevraud by fathers who did not want to pay too much dowry.[42] The second type lived in the Magdalene: Hersende, Petronilla, Agnes and also priests' wives, second-hand spouses, women of easy virtue, and prostitutes.

Robert's design still offered plenty to upset people.

He divided his holy family in the following way: he placed more than 300 women he knew to be virgins in the Great Monastery, and the rest of the female sex he put in the priory of Saint Mary Magdalene. From there, after consulting with others, he afterwards took out the women who had been married and lived with their husbands without reproach, so that they could live with the virgins. So it was that the said priory only housed about 100 or 120 women.

This account comes from a sixteenth-century author, Yves Magistri.[43] It was doubtless at Fontevraud that he heard tell of this mi-

41. Andreas, *Second Life*, chapter 33 (PL 162: 1073; Venarde, *Robert of Arbrissel*, 44).

42. It was standard practice for the family of anyone joining a monastery to offer an entry gift, sometimes referred to as a monastic dowry. According to an old (and still debatable) generalization, it was cheaper to place a daughter in a religious house than to provide a marriage portion; see Venarde, *Women's Monasticism*, 115. There emerged across the twelfth century widespread concern that entry gifts were a form of simony, and by the early thirteenth century women's houses were being singled out as simoniacal. See Joseph H. Lynch, *Simoniacal Entry into Religious Life from 1000 to 1260* (Columbus, OH, 1976), 193–194.

43. Yves Magistri, *Baston de deffence et mirouer des professeurs de la vie reguliere de l'Abbaye et Ordre de Fontevraud* (Angers, 1586), 44.

gration about which other sources are silent. It is illuminating; reading it shows why, since the beginning, the distribution of women between the two establishments lay in shadow. Under new pressures at Fontevraud, hierarchy reasserted its rights. Social segregation was substituted for moral categorization. To read between Magistri's lines, it appears that noblewomen went back to the Great Monastery, perhaps abandoning the Magdalene to the prostitutes and especially to the humble, an operation difficult to justify in the troops of *Pauperes Christi*. This memory to which Magistri was privy arranged things nicely, loose women in one place, great ladies in another. Prostitution legitimized social segregation, clothing it in morality. The procedure avoided the necessity of admitting that the rich did not want to live too long among the poor. By successive corrections, order was restored.

Curiosity remains unsatisfied on one point. Of the women he attracted and gathered to himself, which did Robert cherish and which did he torment? In any case it is not hard to guess from what quarter Geoffrey heard complaints. Robert encouraged noblewomen to scorn their nobility; to make sure, he involved them in everyday matters. Their pride suffered. Geoffrey of Vendôme was their kin, their ally, first cousin to Petronilla of Chemillé. He made himself the spokesman for the women of his world, concluded Jean-Marc Bienvenu.[44] Could it have been Ermengarde of Brittany who denounced the ill-treatment she endured during her short retreat in 1106, in response to Geoffrey's reproaches when she deserted the monastic life?[45] On the other hand, if a unique category of religious women suffered Robert's rebuff, why would Geoffrey have not clearly specified which one? Perhaps Robert's temper did not

---

44. Bienvenu, *L'étonnant fondateur de Fontevraud*, 91–92.

45. This scolding letter to Ermengarde is edited and translated into French in Geoffrey of Vendôme, *Œuvres*, 142–143 (Letter 75); Latin text only in PL 157: 205 (Book 5, Letter 23).

obey any law, changing frequently. Can one not imagine him at turns harsh and tender with an Ermengarde or a Bertrade?

Asking who was treated with favor or bullying takes us away from Robert and loses sight of an obvious fact. The founder of Fontevraud maintained fundamentally ambiguous relations with the women in his entourage, always swinging between the two pedagogical extremes of the cane and the caress. Geoffrey made himself a mirror of this ambivalence, reflecting a reverse image when he tried in turn to dissuade Robert from both familiarity and harshness. "It is through woman that sin entered into the world and through her that all men die. . . . The female sex is quite fragile and delicate, and therefore it must be ruled with the sweetness of compassion more than with excessive severity, lest it be over-whelmed by excessive sorrow." Once again, in this case in a strik-ing fashion, the accuser and the accused speak the same language.

In the absence of intimate revelations from Robert, we can turn to the imagery, to the bestiaries, that Marbode and Geoffrey offer to know what images of women inhabited his spirit.[46] The de-fender of the weaker sex, the "knight errant of monasticism," could not escape the general opinion of his age. First, he feared women, like all men of his class, clerical or lay. For the clergy, they were all the more frightening for the distance from which they were imag-ined. Laymen close to them also put women somewhat aside so that they could remain mysterious and formidable, sorceresses, power-ful poisoners as crafty as Satan. In another letter, Geoffrey wrote that "this detestable sex poisoned our first parent, who was also her husband and her father. It strangled John the Baptist. It deliv-ered the mighty Samson over to his enemies. In a sense, it even killed our Savior, since if sin had not demanded it, he would not

---

46. The bestiary is a genre of medieval literature that describes various ani-mals ("beasts")—often imaginary or mythological ones—and offers allegorical in-terpretations of their qualities as a means of moral or religious instruction.

have needed to die for us. . . . Woe to this sex that has neither fear, nor shame, nor goodness, nor friendliness, that must be more feared when loved than when hated."[47] In Robert's eyes, woman is like the sketch Marbode provided: a lion's head, a dragon's tail, and a body of fire. That is why he chose to go on exposing himself to this flame as the most perilous of punishments.

Deeper in these men's souls, another force was at work, trying with great difficulty to exorcise the chimeras. Marbode, Geoffrey, and doubtless also Robert drew from the scattered material of their culture an attempt to suppress this raging figure of Eve. Mary was the best antidote to the venomous woman. Geoffrey professed a passion for the cult of the Virgin. Marbode wrote poems about her and turned to her to confess his faults, sure of finding comfort and pardon at her breast. Robert dedicated the most important church at Fontevraud to her. There was also another figure, blurry and polymorphous: Mary the sinner, or Magdalene. Geoffrey, in a sermon and a hymn, forgot his rancor at the daughters of Eve to celebrate Mary Magdalene. Robert dedicated another part of Fontevraud to her. Classical Latin authors also made their contribution when Marbode addressed the great ladies Ermengarde of Brittany and Queen Mathilda; and after writing a dread-filled poem on the *meretrix*, he drew on Proverbs to sing the virtues of the *matrona*: what treasure is greater than a good wife?[48]

Beyond this jumble of old and new ideas were Robert's actions. In the woods, during his wanderings, one imagines him on tenterhooks, clenching his teeth against women. This is not beyond what Geoffrey evokes, but also includes familiarity, a hesitant kindness, and the talk that in itself restores confidence, never-ending discussions.

47. Geoffrey of Vendôme, *Œuvres*, 2–5, at pp. 4–5 (Letter 1) or PL 157: 168 (Book 4, Letter 24).

48. Marbode's two poems on women are translated in Alcuin Blamires, *Woman Defamed and Woman Defended: An Anthology of Medieval Texts* (Oxford, 1992),

THE ETERNAL FEMININE?

Robert of Arbrissel had come a long way from Brittany, the land of his origins to which he had long dreamed of returning as a fulfillment, but one whose harshness he now sensed keenly. "You live among barbaric and rude men," he wrote to Ermengarde, an exile from Anjou.[49] He had followed the opposite trajectory. No longer playing at eternal recurrence, Robert went forward without hindrance, cut off from his roots, wherever his feet took him.[50] In departure from La Roë and in settlement at Fontevraud, he moved from the extreme north to the extreme south of Anjou. La Roë was at the border of Brittany, Fontevraud facing Poitou and Aquitaine, where William IX ruled as count and duke.

Several times already, Robert's story has crossed William's. Who was he? The seventh count of Poitou and ninth duke of Aquitaine by that name, he took the titles in 1086, not yet fifteen years old, the double inheritance of his father, although he, too, was a William the Bastard.[51] Between 1089 and 1091, he was perhaps married to Ermengarde of Anjou, but then renounced her. He took as his second wife Philippa of Toulouse, widow of the king of Aragon, which encouraged his designs on the county of Toulouse. In 1101 he went on crusade, going along in support of new Chris-

---

100–103 (*De meretrice*) and 228–232 (*De matrona*). The biblical reference is Prv 31:10–11. In both poems Marbode cites instances from ancient history and mythology treated by classical Latin writers.

49. Jules de Pétigny, "Lettre inédite de Robert d'Arbrissel à la comtesse Ermengarde," *Bibliothèque de l'Ecole des Chartes* 15 (1854), 228; Venarde, *Robert of Arbrissel*, 75.

50. "Eternal recurrence" is a concept developed by the philosopher Friedrich Nietzsche, the notion that all that is happening now has already gone on for an eternity in the past and will happen for an eternity in the future. Time is infinite, then, but experience and material things are not.

51. Pope Gregory VII had ordered William VIII to disown his third wife, the future William IX's mother, by reason of consanguinity. By one set of standards, then, the marriage was invalid and its progeny illegitimate.

tian kingdoms in the East. He experienced setbacks, ambushes, storms, and returned defeated to Poitiers. Seized by frenzy, he flaunted mistresses, taunted the Church, bawled bawdiness, issuing his *gab*, his boastful challenge, for a duel of a different sort.

> On a fine cushion
> I know all the games to play. . . .
> I know more about it than anyone around
> As you can see for yourself. . . .
> I go by "Infallible Master."
> No girlfriend will ever have me for a night
> Who won't want me again the next day.
> I am—I brag about it—
> So well trained in this craft
> That I can earn my daily bread by it
> In any market.

It is as if, by this unbridled virility, he was trying to forget his losses. He simply prepared others for himself. The women of Aquitaine and Poitou, Anjou and Toulouse as well, were perhaps a little freer than those elsewhere, accustomed to the refinement of the southern courts, with their influence among dynasties. William saw his former wife and his new one in turn look toward Fontevraud, toward the apostle who discovered, in their parlance, unknown accents. He was shaken and defended himself, badly, threatening to roast any woman who turned away from a loyal knight to love a monk or a cleric.

> The lady commits a grave and mortal sin
> Who loves not a loyal knight
> But if she loves a monk or cleric
> She had lost her mind.
> It's just that she should be burned
> With a brand.

The historian Reto R. Bezzola thinks that this rivalry between Robert and William, the priest and the knight, for the favors of noble ladies was a decisive stage in the origins of chivalric literature.[52] More than one piece of evidence supports his case. The chronicler William of Malmesbury reports a surprising foundation by the duke of Aquitaine:

In the region of Niort he built a house on the model of a small monastery, saying in his madness that he was founding an abbey for prostitutes and repeating that he was going to name this or that woman abbess or prioress or other official according to how celebrated they were in the whore's art.[53]

There is a good chance that the duke dreamt this up as a satire and also as an accusation, a sacrilegious replica of Fontevraud. In the end, though, after all his (doubtless vain) efforts, he chose to enter into rivalry with Robert's spiritual mysticism by means of a worldly mysticism. Thus he merited the title of "the first troubadour."

> You are whiter than ivory,
> Which is why I adore no other.
> If I do not find help soon
> So that my beautiful lady will love me
> I'll die, by Saint Gregory's head,
> If she does not kiss me in the bedchamber or under leafy boughs.
>
> Our love goes along
> Like a hawthorn's branch
> Trembling on the tree
> Left out at night in rain and cold.
> But the next day the sun shines
> On the limb's green leaves.[54]

52. Reto R. Bezzola, *Les origines et la formation de la littérature courtoise en Occident (500–1200)*, 3 vols. (Paris, 1944–1963), 2: 275–292.

53. William of Malmesbury, *Gesta Regum Anglorum* 1: 782–785 (section 439), translation adapted slightly.

54. On the four sections of verse in the last few pages see *The Poetry of William VII, Count of Poitiers, IX Duke of Aquitaine*, ed. and trans. Gerald A. Bond (New York, 1982), 24–27, 18–19, 44–45, and 36–37 (in the order of poems quoted). Dalarun translated the first, third, and fourth excerpts into modern French, leav-

Marbode, Geoffrey, William, and Robert shed light on one another. They have the same fear, the same desire for the female
flame, plus something else that still has no name.

---

ing the second in its original Occitan. I have translated all into English, referring
to Bond's edition and translation.

4

FACES

The women were dreams that took on bodily form. That is to say they lack the essential: faces, the play of looks that peer at each other, defining, more than any outline or list of traits, the irreplaceable individuality of each being. From the two *vitae* we have with some effort extracted only three female first names: Hersende, Petronilla, and Agnes. The rest of the women who crowded around at the master's call remain anonymous masses, fuel for the ordeal's bonfire and recruits for the nuns' brigade.

So we must have recourse to the lesser known pieces of the dossier in order that these silhouettes become more defined, that their forms come to life, and that the masses disperse and separate into living beings. Documents tell of four encounters, all apparently dating from the last years of Robert of Arbrissel's life. At the end of a long journey, the meetings signal a new calm. They demanded it, too; Robert was forced for a moment to forget himself and his self-hatred, forget to punish himself, so that he could plunge into the sea of faces that opened up and offered themselves to him. Is there a risk that the first of these encounters, in the warmth of a brothel, places him in the clutches of women who, having long sold their bodies, no longer possess anything of their own but their glances, which cannot be bought?

THE PROSTITUTES OF ROUEN

One day, passing through Rouen, he entered a brothel, and, sitting down near the hearth to warm his feet, he was surrounded by prostitutes who thought he had come to have sex. Instead he preaches the words of life and promises the mercy of Christ to them. One of the prostitutes, who was in charge of the others, says to him, "Who are you to talk this way? Take my word for it: in the twenty-five years since I came into this house to perpetrate wickedness, never has anyone come in here to speak of God or give us hope in His mercy. Yet if I knew what you say were true, I swear to you, by Christ whom I have wearied with my innumerable sins, I would renounce them gladly!" Robert replies to her, "Have faith, my daughter, and do not lose hope in His mercy. For if you renounce sin and follow my sound advice, you will without a doubt gain God's mercy." At these words, the prostitute falls at once at his feet, along with the others who lived there. They promise to renounce their sins and do penance in good works. Immediately the holy man leads them from the city to the wilderness to carry on his journey rejoicing with them and he took pleasure in passing over in silence his act of benefaction. . . .[1]

The text is stunning for its vivid daring, but its authenticity is uncertain. It begins vaguely ("one day") and ends in suspended animation, at the point of escape from the depths of a brothel, before the curtain falls. We have no medieval manuscript of the story. It was passed down by two seventeenth-century scholars who edited it in Latin in their histories of Fontevraud, removed from all context, amidst a jumble of sundry documents. One scholar dates it to the twelfth century, the other to 1210; neither names an author. What trust can we accord this testimony? In a brief introduction, the more learned of the two scholars and doubtless the better informed claims that he received a copy of the text taken directly from the original, a manuscript from the abbey of Vaux-de-Cernay. He adds that its author was surely a contemporary of Robert of Ar-

---

1. Latin text in Dalarun, *L'impossible sainteté*, 349.

brissel. The track is faint, but it allows the formulation of a few hypotheses.[2]

In 1118, a small group of monks founded the abbey of Vaux-de-Cernay in a hollow of the Chevreuse Valley.[3] They were followers of Vitalis of Savigny. This friend of Robert's, another prince of the hermits of western France, had founded a monastic order in Normandy and sought to extend it into new territories; hence the arrival in the Ile-de-France of this band, which had been sent forth from the motherhouse. Vitalis, Robert, and Bernard of Tiron together crisscrossed the western French lands to call crowds to a change of life. That their steps one day took them to Rouen and one of their followers saw or heard about the scene where Robert had made himself known to the prostitutes is not improbable. One must thus imagine a follower and witness who settled among the disciples of Vitalis and who eventually departed Savigny for Vaux-de-Cernay. Before his death, he recorded the most glorious exploits he witnessed in his youth while following these wandering spiritual athletes of bygone days. This hypothesis is strengthened by a note in the *Life of Vitalis* that he, too, labored to tear prostitutes away from their "vile trade." To gain their confidence, Vitalis called them "by the sweet name of 'daughters'" and lavished them with "sweet embraces."[4] Although we have previously expressed doubt that all the repentant women who took refuge at Fontevraud were prostitutes, here it is clear that many of Vitalis's recruits, like Robert's, were indeed sex workers. The two friends shared the same care for lost daughters, the same gentleness in taming them, the same call to a new life.

There is no full study about the place of prostitution in

2. On the history of the text, see Dalarun, *L'impossible saintété*, 345–346.

3. Vaux-de-Cernay is not far from Paris, to the south-southwest. Substantial remains of the twelfth-century buildings exist today.

4. Etienne de Fougères, *Vita B. Vitalis*, ed. E.-P. Sauvage, *Analecta Bollandiana* 1 (1882), 365.

eleventh- and twelfth-century society. We need one.[5] It could be that one of the functions of the era's reviving towns was to provide a red-light district for those passing through and for the surrounding countryside. So our text would suggest; Robert pushes open the first door he comes to in order to find a little warmth and there he is, in a brothel. The entire scene is marked by a naturalness that inspires faith in the text's authenticity: the hearth where the penitent seeks to warm up the bare feet that indicate his profession, the confusion of the women who take him for a client, the subsequent dialogue, the verbs that pass into the present tense when the action becomes clearer or speeds up—all that sounds true.

This realistic, zesty text, crackling with life, is nevertheless a cento, a literary patchwork composed of extracts from earlier writings. At least two guiding threads intertwine in it, the New Testament and the Lives of the Egyptian fathers, which furnish the author the warp and weft of his text. First there is a short text from the East, which in time would inspire Anatole France and Jules Massenet. To save the sinner Thaïs, the holy man Paphnutius puts on secular garb, goes to her house, and pays her as if he means to transact sexual business. It turns out he is there to exhort her to repentance. He snatches her away from vice and shuts her up in a tiny cell, sealing the door shut with lead.[6] In another extract from the "Egyptian matter," a monk in Alexandria makes a list of all the

5. In the twenty years since Dalarun made this remark, a handful of local and regional studies of medieval prostitution have appeared, including Ruth Mazo Karras, *Common Women: Prostitution and Sexuality in Medieval England* (New York, 1996). A brief survey is Jacques Rossiaud, *Medieval Prostitution*, trans. Lydia G. Cochrane (New York, 1988). It remains the case that there is no study focused on prostitution in eleventh- and twelfth-century Europe.

6. On Thaïs and Paphnutius, see Benedicta Ward, *Harlots of the Desert: A Study of Repentance in Early Monastic Sources* (Kalamazoo, MI, 1987), 76–84, with a translation of the Latin version of the *Life of Thaïs* with which Robert and his contemporaries would have been familiar, 83–84. Anatole France used the story as the basis of a novel (in 1890), Jules Massenet for an opera (in 1894).

town's prostitutes. He goes to the house of each, one by one, and says, "Give me this night and do not fornicate!" He spends the night in a corner of their rooms awake in prayer. In the eyes of the world, however, he fosters confusion by announcing far and wide that he is on his way to the house of so-and-so, who is waiting for him. To the scandalized he replies, "Have I not a body like everyone else? Are monks not like other men? Mind your own business!"[7]

So the story of Robert's entrance into the brothel, a combination of daring and provocation, has literary precedent in the holy fools of Egypt; but the conversion of prostitutes finds its source even further upstream, in a passage from the Gospels where a sinner falls at the feet of Christ, washes them with her tears, dries them with her hair, covers them with kisses, and anoints them with perfume.[8] Falling at the feet of their guest, the women of Rouen recall this scene. Furthermore, the mercy Robert promises is a true copy of the remission of sins carried out by Christ, while the expression "Have faith, my daughter" duplicates the words of the Lord to the bleeding woman.[9] Moreover, it is not just to these literary texts that the story refers. To pass from damnation to salvation, it is necessary to leave the city for the wilderness. Which one? Rouen, the real or symbolic city, "the great Babylon, mother of the repulsive prostitutes of the world," whose imminent punishment Revelation announces?[10]

Analyzed this way, the Rouen text appears to lose all three-dimensionality, all vitality: a pure literary construction, a collage of commonplaces, from which to construct an edifying anecdote, a roundabout sermon for sleepy listeners, but containing nothing au-

---

7. Vitalis, a monk of Gaza, is said to have gone to Alexandria at age 60 on a mission to convert all the city's prostitutes but without telling anyone his mission, giving rise to great suspicion. His brief *vita* is edited in AASS, January, volume 1, 702–703.

8. Lk 7:36–38. 9. Mt 9:20–22.

10. Rev 17:5.

thentic about Robert of Arbrissel. Historical episode or literary construction? Where we would see a clear choice, the Middle Ages did not necessarily discern a contradiction. In this era, text and experience had relations the reverse of those we assign them. Writing, we believe, has the purpose of relating (more or less imperfectly) what has happened. The account sails along behind the course of events, always in its wake, trying to record what occurs. Failing that, it leads us into another universe, that of fiction. By contrast, in medieval thought, at least to Robert's time, words were not content to express things; they were the sole reality of them. God created the world by speaking it. The Word dictates the event.

This truth, endlessly repeated by schoolmasters, was what saints' Lives were meant to fulfill with every page. Here is the fertile ambiguity of the term *vita*, at once writing and existence. The Life of a saint is a text woven of many earlier texts that the saint revives or which, rather, drive him along at every step, since writing is the source of life. This philosophical truth firmly set in the minds of clerics thus by necessity became a psychological truth. Consequently we need not automatically doubt the historicity of a scene even when it seems made up of literary echoes. When Robert, perhaps by chance, entered a Rouen dive, he was so molded by the example of the desert fathers that he could do no other than follow the path of Paphnutius; or perhaps he entered as a challenge, so as to be covered in disgrace like the monk of Alexandria. Model and imitator, seven or eight centuries apart, were not separate in spirit but joined by the Apostle's idea: "Yes, I am glad in my weaknesses, in insults, distresses, persecutions, and anguish endured for Christ; for when I am weak, it is then I am strong."[11]

Every saint recalls the virtues of a previous saint and all attempt to revive the virtues of Christ, the crucible from which they all come and in which they will all merge. In the final analysis, the

11. 2 Cor 12:10.

commonplace of all hagiography is that by nature it cannot be anything other than a literature of commonplaces. Each of God's fools found another even more foolish in Egypt, and none of them could equal the folly of the cross. Like a desert father, like Christ, Robert was not really acting a part. He was not playing or disguising himself in someone else. He was celebrating, just as the priest celebrates the mystery of the Mass.

I think what is reported actually happened at Rouen. However, the scribe who bore witness, either because he saw it happen or because someone recounted it as truth, was also subject to the omnipotence of the Word. To relate an event consisted above all, in his mind, of recalling earlier texts that he felt had dictated it. Perhaps he might reshape a snatch of dialogue or an attitude a little bit in order to make his hero conform more closely to Christ or the prostitute to the beloved sinner of the Gospel. Should we then accuse him of being unfaithful to the truth? On the contrary: he was convinced he was putting it right, elevating it. After recounting how Vitalis of Savigny took care to extirpate prostitutes' baseness, his hagiographer shows the motive as being nothing other than the fulfillment of Scripture. "By Gospel testimony, we know that tax-collectors and sinners were welcomed by our Lord, that the possessed were cured and the sick delivered from their infirmities. And now we know that through the care of this servant of Christ, prostitutes were dragged away from the hideous abyss of their cursed work and given over to conjugal chastity by his authority and with his advice. For He who once relieved suffering by His own hand now acts through His servant."[12]

A literary hall of mirrors, hagiography often makes its reader despair of extracting biography from it. A *vita* seems to blow out of all proportion an extraordinary person and is, in fact, a radical

12. Etienne de Fougères, *Vita B. Vitalis* [*Life of the Blessed Vitalis*], ed. E.-P. Sauvage, *Analecta Bollandiana* 1 (1882), 365.

negation of individuality. In the sense we understand it today, the individual did not exist until the later Middle Ages. John Scotus Erigena, a jewel of the Carolingian Renaissance, repeated after Dionysius the Areopagite (who himself assumed that name to remain anonymous) that the universe is a cascade of light that diffuses from the Uncreated One to heavenly and earthly creatures. No mortal shines by his own light. He is instead a vessel and a mirror; the light he receives from the One he reflects back toward the One in a ceaseless surge of praise.[13] What can we grasp about Robert of Arbrissel in this to-ing and fro-ing? Is there any purpose to the enterprise at all?

No single *vita* is an exact replica of the Scripture on which it is based. By virtue of connection to Christ, each of these athletes of God is unique, eccentric in the way that got St. Peter crucified upside down. Each new holy person kept only a few godparents from among the saints who came before; thus there emerge spiritual lineages that diverge little by little from their common origin. Furthermore, there was always a little play in the learned collection of bits and pieces that make up a *vita*, tiny shifts, small deletions. Assessing the saint's peculiarities, recognizing his spiritual affiliations while grasping where he diverges from them, taking advantage of a badly sewn seam, a slack piece in the motley patchwork of a hagiographic text—these processes are our best chances of sniffing out what is now, according to the famous dictate of Marc Bloch, the object of our enquiry: human flesh.[14]

13. John Scotus Erigena (ca. 810–ca. 877) was a theologian who worked for the family of Charlemagne, the Carolingians, specifically Charlemagne's grandson Charles the Bald, a great patron of culture. He translated from Greek into Latin the works of a theologian who identified himself as Dionysius the Areopagite but lived some centuries later than the New Testament convert to Christianity of that name (Acts 17:34). For the material about light and creation, see *Pseudo-Dionysius: The Complete Works*, trans. Colm Luibhéid et al. (New York, 1987), 143–191 ("The Celestial Hierarchy").

14. Marc Bloch (1886–1944) was one the great medievalists of the twentieth

When Thaïs renounced lust, Paphnutius shut her up in a little lead-sealed cell. There was only a small window to allow someone to pass her bread and water. "Where, father, do you want me to urinate?" "In your cell," he replied, "just as you deserve." When she asked him how to pray to God in her tiny refuge, he told her, "You are not worthy to pronounce God's name, nor to have the name of the Trinity on your lips, nor even to lift your hands toward heaven, for your lips are full of sin and your hands covered with filth." It took three years of imprisonment to finish her expiation.[15] In Robert's time, people still used the old Carolingian penitentials that, for each type of offense, indicated with great precision the number of days or years of fasting necessary to obtain the remission of sins.[16] Paphnutius would have found them familiar. Robert did not condemn the lost sheep of Rouen to death in this world, but "preaches the words of life and promises them mercy." Four times the word "mercy" appears in his mouth or theirs—and "hope" twice. The visitor does not ask these women to do penance and it is they, furthermore, who promise it.

When Paphnutius wondered if it was right to release Thaïs, there began a long proceeding under the authority of Anthony, the father of hermits, assisted by Paul of Thebes. It took nothing less than the intervention of an angel of the Lord to sway the learned assembly. Robert delivered women not from three-year penances but a quarter-century of servitude: "In the twenty-five years since I

---

century. Dalarun alludes to a passage in his meditations on historical enquiry written not long before the Nazis executed him for taking part in the French Resistance. "The good historian is like the giant of the fairy tale. He knows that wherever he catches the scent of human flesh, there his quarry lies" (Marc Bloch, *The Historian's Craft*, trans. Peter Putnam [New York, 1953], 26).

15. Ward, *Harlots of the Desert*, 83–84.

16. A "penitential" is a handbook describing various kinds of sins to be confessed and penance to be done for forgiveness. Such manuals date from the earliest period of European Christianity; learned penitentials from the Carolingian era were still used in the twelfth century.

came into this house to perpetrate wickedness, never has anyone come in here to speak of God." The courtesan is doubly stunned, first that anyone speaks to her of God, but perhaps even more that any words at all are addressed to her. Jacques Lacarrière has quite rightly characterized the conversion of Thaïs as "a myth from the time before grace."[17] It seemed to be that time stood still in the brothel at Rouen until Robert came like a breath of spring air.

In Christian tradition, every innovation is a reappearance, like the return of spring. Without ever saying her name, the entire brothel scene evokes the Magdalene. Catholic exegesis subsumed several figures from the Gospels under the identity of Mary of Magdala. She is the nameless sinner who anointed the head or feet of Jesus at Bethany, in the home of Simon the Pharisee.[18] In John's Gospel, she is merged with Mary, the sister of Martha and the resurrected Lazarus,[19] the one who chose the better part because she gave herself up to conversation with the Lord.[20] Finally she is identified with the Mary of Magdala who, along with the holy women, found their crucified Lord's tomb empty,[21] and who was the first to see Christ in the glory of his resurrection.[22] Medieval devotion to this distinguished figure was fervent from the eleventh century at Vézelay,[23] and the imagination of the time further increased her im-

---

17. Lacarrière, *Les hommes ivres de Dieu*, 118. The idea is that Paphnutius made Thaïs pay dearly for her redemption. This is in marked contrast to Robert's attitude; he was confident in the power of the divine gift of grace to redeem sinners without such punishment. I am grateful to Jacques Dalarun for explaining the point.

18. Mt 26:6–7, Lk 7:36–38.   19. Jn 11:1–43.

20. Lk 10:38–42.   21. Mt 28:1–8; Lk 24:1–10.

22. Jn 20:1–18, where Mary of Magdala goes to the tomb alone. In Mt 28:9–10 Jesus appears to both women who visited his tomb, one of whom is Mary of Magdala.

23. Relics said to be the bones of the Magdalene arrived in this Burgundian town around AD 1000; the church built to house them is a landmark of Romanesque architecture.

portance by trying to engage her to John the Evangelist. Her story grew with apocryphal tales that had the Magdalene arriving at the port of Marseilles with Lazarus and Martha. Her brother became bishop of the city while Martha faced down the Tarasque, the eponymous monster of Tarascon.[24] The Magdalene, having taken active part in the evangelization of the region, withdrew to a dreadful wilderness later called Sainte-Baume. She stayed there thirty years, according to legend established in the thirteenth century.[25]

The eremitic branch grafted itself onto the tree of tradition starting in the tenth century and blossomed in the eleventh, when the West went in search of a more human Christ, pondered the Incarnation, and found great enthusiasm for holy places, the surroundings of Jesus' life on earth. In the long process of rediscovering a man-God that would reach its height with St. Francis of Assisi a century after Robert, the cult of the Magdalene was a necessary step, for it was she who touched and embraced Jesus most intimately. In the Rouen brothel, Robert gathered together in one scene layers of legend and gave them shape. He brought the pardon that Christ had given the sinner "because she had shown great love."[26] Then he led the converts to the desert. We should not imagine them undergoing either the ill-treatment endured by Thaïs or indeed any inflicted by Robert himself. The desert of the

24. Tarascon is on the Rhône River, north of Marseilles. Legend has it that Martha heard from the people of the town about this half-animal and half-fish creature that terrorized river traffic and the surrounding countryside, eating sheep and people. Martha tamed the monster and led it back to town, where the citizens promptly killed it.

25. In the thirteenth century, a grotto thought to be the Magdalene's home and bones in an early Christian sarcophagus were discovered at Sainte-Baume, in central Provence. Pilgrimage to these two sites grew; Charles of Anjou (1227–1285), younger brother of the saintly King Louis IX of France, sponsored the construction of a large Gothic church to house the relics.

26. Lk 7:47.

Magdalene was not a jail for expiation but rather a mountain pass, a place of rapture, for seven times a day angels lifted it toward heaven to contemplate in glory the One loved so much here below.[27]

Vitalis of Savigny joined his friend in concern for these lost souls but did not share Robert's boldness. Vitalis found husbands for the women he tore away from their "vile trade," assembling a dowry from alms. Everything went back to normal. For the prostitutes freed from the Rouen brothel, though, fate led them to increase the scandalous troop that stretched out impulsively in the forest. Robert was far closer than Vitalis to the fool of Alexandria who asked the prostitutes only for one night of abstinence. "Word has it you say one night suffices for you to prevent sin."[28] That is Marbode of Rennes speaking in reproach to Robert of Arbrissel. Marbode's criticism gives the key to the Rouen episode and gauges its true daring: spiritual daring. Unlike Paphnutius, Carolingian penetentials, or Marbode, the hermit did not believe there was anything irreparable about sin, nor even any method of drawing up accounts for it. For Robert, each sin was original since divine mercy would know how to bind up the wound and bring back the lost sheep to its primordial innocence from before the Fall. Everyone is his own Adam and Christ is for all.

Michelet loved these spiritual fireworks and as an intellectual struggled so that man could be "his own Prometheus." He sensed so acutely the importance of this misunderstood text that he centered his study of the founder of Fontevraud on the unique incident in the Rouen brothel, disregarding the other sources. He saw in it, beyond Robert, the tipping-point of the fate of women in the West:

27. The seven elevations refer to the seven daily prayer services (along with one at night) of monastic tradition, the *opus Dei*, the work of God.

28. Walter, *Die ersten Wanderprediger Frankreichs*, 2: 188 and PL 171: 1484; Venarde, *Robert of Arbrissel*, 98.

"Grace prevailing over law, there emerged, quite noticeably, a great religious revolution. God changed sex, so to speak." Even if his disregard for other sources led to some ill-considered excesses in his analysis, Michelet's intuition was remarkable.[29] At Rouen, Robert did indeed set off an earthquake whose aftershocks reach us still today, a novelty entirely expressed through the interplay of very old texts. Under the threadbare patches of his clothing were some of real life's palpitations.

ERMENGARDE

The spirit of pride is an evil, but the pretense of humility is worse. The spirit of vainglory is an evil, but the pretense of sanctity is worse. The spirit of envy is an evil, but the pretense of love is worse. The spirit of greed is an evil, but the pretense of mercy is worse. The spirit of gluttony is an evil, but the pretense of abstinence is worse. The spirit of lust is an evil, but the pretense of chastity is worse. Handmaid of Christ, beware these evils heard and known, manifest or pretended! For virtue is a middle ground between opposing vices. See that you do nothing to excess: everything excessive is turned into vice.[30]

Here Marbode of Rennes could be proud of his student. These remarks are those of Robert himself in a long letter of direction addressed to Countess Ermengarde of Brittany. Written between 1106 and 1109 but forgotten until the nineteenth century, the letter was edited then by Jules de Pétigny. The account he gives of the romantic life of the countess should be read with caution, but what

29. Michelet, *Œuvres complètes* 4: 13, 460. On Michelet's discussion of Robert of Arbrissel, see Dalarun, *L'impossible sainteté*, 120–134.

30. Jules de Pétigny, "Lettre inédite de Robert d'Arbrissel à la comtesse Ermengarde," *Bibliothèque de l'Ecole des Chartes* 15 (1854): 225–235, is the full text of the letter translated in Venarde, *Robert of Arbrissel*, 68–79. The sentences here open the only known text (except for the statutes of Fontevraud) written by Robert himself (Pétigny, "Lettre inédite de Robert d'Arbrissel," 225; Venarde, *Robert of Arbrissel*, 73).

stands up to analysis is sufficient to show that such a call to moderation was timely.

Ermengarde was the daughter of Count Fulk le Réchin of Anjou and his first wife, the daughter of Lancelot of Beaugency. She was born around 1069 and raised in the brilliant court of Angers, famous for its poets and learned men. Ermengarde was possibly forced into the bed of William of Aquitaine, but if the marriage ever took place, it was short-lived by reason of consanguinity. This age evidently had a finicky notion of incest; two of the spouses' great-grandparents were brother and sister. This was kinship in the sixth degree, but clerics extended the prohibition to the seventh generation (the fourteenth degree in our current calculation), and the powerful found in it an excuse to discard their spouses.[31] Around 1092, Ermengarde was already (re)wed to Alan Fergent, the count of Brittany. Early in their marriage, she conceived two sons and a daughter. When he left for five years in the Holy Land in 1096, Ermengarde governed Brittany. The Crusades, from this perspective, increased the power of aristocratic women, even if it was for the most part delegated power.

Ermengarde would play a very active role in the guidance of Breton affairs her whole life. Even so, she did not love the land. For a girl raised in Anjou, what Michelet called "soft and sensual country," "poor and harsh" Brittany offered a sorry contrast. Robert, in his letter, offers a fearsome description:

Teachers, bishops, abbots, and simoniacal priests, princes who are wicked rapists, adulterers and the incestuous, a people that does not know God's law. Nobody does good, nobody speaks good, everyone contradicts the truth. There is neither truth, nor mercy, nor knowledge in that land. Falsehood, adultery, and murder have overflowed and bloodshed follows bloodshed.

31. On the new emphasis on kinship and incest, see chapter 2. It appears that marriage between Ermengarde and the future troubadour count was arranged, but it is not clear it was ever consummated.

One need be only partly moved, though. If the setbacks of the one-time archpriest could inspire the beginning of this diatribe, the end reproduces the prophet Hosea's reproaches of the children of Israel.[32] Nonetheless there is other evidence that depicts the Brittany of the time in a harsh light. Marbode of Rennes claimed that nobody could leave home in his episcopal city without being beaten by thieves.[33]

A land of such brutality was hardly the place for Ermengarde, who had developed a taste for the praise of poets.

> Daughter of Count Fulk, ornament of Brittany,
> Beautiful, chaste, decent, famous, fresh, and bright,
> If you had not passed to the marital bed
> And to childbirth's hard labor,
> You would be, in my view, a Cynthia.[34]
> But since chastity is worth more than marriage
> And virginity is a greater honor still,
> You seem like a goddess of the first order among wives
> You who are so beautiful!
> But this beauty, o daughter and wife of princes,
> Will pass into smoke and soon be cinders.
> Or if your end is delayed by destiny
> Then, hideous crime, you will be an old woman.
> Your beautiful face is celebrated and it is precious,
> But death or old age will destroy its worth.
> Your luminous gaze that wounds those around you
> And your blond hair will both become ashes.
> You are reputed to have no equal
> In your powerful eloquence and wise counsel,
> But all that will pass for nothing but fable. . . .
> The riches of the world will endure for no one.

32. Pétigny, "Lettre inédite de Robert d'Arbrissel," 228; Venarde, *Robert of Arbrissel*, 75. The last three sentences are a rephrasing of Hos 4:1–2.

33. Marbode savaged his adopted city in a short poem "Urbs Redonensis" (PL 171: 1726–1727).

34. Cynthia is an alternate name for Artemis (Roman Diana), the classical goddess of the moon, the hunt, and chastity.

> They pass with the world and fall away with it.
> To love Jesus Christ and despise the world
> To act as clothing and food for the poor—
> That will make you beautiful and precious to the Savior,
> a worth neither age nor death will destroy.[35]

Ermengarde would have been about thirty when a skilled poet familiar with Latin classics—probably Marbode, former master of the cathedral school at Angers—addressed this very Epicurean piece to her. The irony is delicious. At the same time the spiritual guide pretends to instruct the princess to scorn the world, the courtier renders exaggerated homage to the mature beauty of one who was, like him, a companion in exile in Brittany. About 1106, she could not bear it there. She fled and took refuge, it seems, at Fontevraud. Perhaps she sincerely hoped, as Robert put it, "naked to follow the naked Christ on the cross." Still, he knew as well that she was trying to escape a place she despised and a faithless husband. Taking her cue from men of her class, she tried to discover a blood relationship to Count Alan. Unfortunately, "By ecclesiastical judgment, you cannot be separated from your husband. You have done what you could; you fled. The Church brought you back." Robert specifies the reasons for failure: "You did not find witnesses willing to furnish proof." He means proofs of consanguinity, genealogies that some learned old man would have explained publicly. Perhaps the count of Brittany had managed to obscure memories somewhat in order to keep his wife under his control.

So Ermengarde went back to her court. Immediately, Geoffrey of Vendôme, who never missed a chance to lecture someone, scolded her for this desertion. Why did she allow herself to be snatched up by the "false happiness" of the world, this "creature for whom the Author of Life died?"[36] The import of a letter Robert sent to his

---

35. PL 171: 1659–1660.

36. For the letter to Ermengarde quoted in this paragraph, see Geoffrey of

onetime guest at Fontevraud is entirely different. He exhorts her to stay in the world united to her faithless husband, to attend the standard seven daily prayer services (what he considered "short prayers"), and to practice hidden virtue in the form of interior piety. On one particular point, Robert is very insistent. "Seek by any means to obtain your daughter's separation. Otherwise, always carry grief in your heart for so despicable a deed!" Hedwig, Alan and Ermengarde's daughter, had been engaged to the son of Count Robert II of Flanders. Robert's letter says that the girl had been "handed over to death." Was it because the two were related in the twelfth degree, an obstacle sufficiently serious that Pope Pascal II chose to break the engagement? Or was it because of the ferociousness of the heir to Flanders, called Baldwin the Ax "because he always carried a battle-ax that he also used in his office as executioner"?[37] More than one marriage of his era had the character of a burnt offering. There is no record of how Ermengarde received Robert's admonitions. Apparently they did not dislodge her obsession with spiritual seeking.

In 1112, at the end of a grave illness, Count Alan decided to retire to the abbey of Redon. Jules de Pétigny speculated that Ermengarde took advantage of this development to return to Fontevraud when her son Conan came of age and secured his hold on power. Did Ermengarde prepare to enjoy a happy retirement at Robert's side? Was it the master's death that freed her from her vows? In any case, Ermengarde went back to the life of the court, taking part in all decisions and assemblies. She governed in her son's name while her husband, true to his vow, died in 1119 without ever leaving the monastery.

In 1130, when Ermengarde had passed sixty, she met Bernard

Vendôme, *Œuvres*, 142–143 (Letter 75; with French translation) or PL 157: 205 (Book 5, Letter 23).

37. Pétigny, "Lettre inédite de Robert d'Arbrissel," 219–220.

of Clairvaux. As had once happened with Robert, she was captivated by the powerful voice of a great reformer. She took the veil at the priory of Larrey from Bernard's own hands and a correspondence began.

> Oh, if you could read on my heart the love for you that God deigned to inscribe there with His own finger, you would surely know that no tongue and no pen can suffice to express what the spirit of God has been able to imprint in the very marrow of my bones. I am now with you in thought although absent in body. But how I seem does not depend on you or me. Yet you have the means, failing certain knowledge, to assess if what I say is true. Enter into your heart and look at mine. Grant that I have as much love toward you as you have for me. And if you presume to believe that you love more and I love less, do not judge yourself superior to me by believing that you have surmounted me in charity.[38]

Bernard wrote these lines and it requires a moment of digression to square them with the grand figure of the abbot of Clairvaux. It was Bernard, after all, who showed the need to convert self-love into love of community, which is compassion for one's neighbor. He argued that carnal love, whose trembling is evident in this letter, should be quickly passed over in the degrees of charity as nothing more than the first step toward mystical marriage.[39] In 1132, Bernard went far away and Ermengarde departed for the East. She spent two years there and then returned to Brittany where, again forsaking her vows, she resumed her place at court at her son's side. In 1147, nearly eighty years old, she died in the part of the world she had once been so desperate to escape.

In the sermon that had, forty years earlier, encouraged Ermengarde to remain in Brittany, Robert tells us about not only Ermengarde but also himself. Again, these are not confidential remarks.

---

38. PL 182: 262–263. For a less literal translation, see *The Letters of Saint Bernard of Clairvaux*, trans. Bruno Scott James (Kalamazoo, MI, 1998), 181.

39. This is the theme of Bernard of Clairvaux's short treatise *On Loving God (De diligendo Deo)*, of which there are several English translations.

In a letter contained on but two manuscript folios, there are fifty-two references to Scripture. The manner in which they cluster around a few key points tells a great deal.

With the first words, Robert puts himself in the camp of *discretio*, as if Marbode's lessons hit home. "There are many hypocritical clerics, monks, and hermits who, in order to please men, pretend to make long prayers to be seen by men. . . . Exercise *discretio* in everything, in abstinence, fasting, vigils, and prayers." After prohibiting excess austerity in diet, the spiritual director adds, "The kingdom of God is not in food and drink but in grace and peace." Robert did not, for all that, turn into a mediocre defender of creature comfort and the social order. Moderation in appearances is not a goal in itself but the price of admission to interior piety. "Whether you are in the city, at court, in your ivory bed, in splendid clothing, in the army, sitting in judgment, or feasting, keep God in your heart!" Do not flee the world, do not even accord it the honor of scorn, but live in trust of God. "Amidst positions and honors, riches and silk garments, alongside your husband and dear children and splendid parent, sighing along with the prophet say 'I am a poor beggar and the Lord keeps watch over me.'"[40] The only asceticism fitting to impose must be invisible and cheerful; it consists primarily of Ermengarde embracing her fate and, especially, her husband. "You live for the time being among savage men. Flee their wicked works in your heart. . . . True patience is that conquered by no rage, weakened by no tribulation." Far from spectacular acts of self-mortification, this is a return to the hairshirt concealed beneath splendid clothing.

At the same time he preached moderation, an irrepressible force led Robert to his old delight, the pleasure of excess. The series of shifts in his thought are very important. Moderation is equity, and equity is the justice that validates proper punishments for

40. See Ps 39/40:18.

criminals. '"Blessed are those who keep judgment and do justice always.' And in the Gospel, 'Blessed are those who hunger and thirst for justice.' Again, 'Blessed are those who suffer persecution for justice.'"[41] This is the first slip: passing the bar, the calm judge finds himself accused and unjustly persecuted. Amidst barbarians, Ermengarde must take refuge in the peace of her heart, to know secret triumph and rejoicing. "As the Gospel says, 'You will be blessed when men hate you, curse you, reproach you, and ban your name as wicked because of me. Rejoice and be triumphant, for your reward will be great in heaven.' And again, 'If the world hates you, know that it hated me first. . . . If they have called the father Beelzebub, what would they not call His servants?'"[42] Finally, exhorting his addressee to find help in the Lord, Robert offers, "For it is written, 'God whips every son He receives' and 'Blessed is the man chastened by God.' And in Revelation, 'Those whom I love I rebuke and correct.'"[43]

The meeting of Robert of Arbrissel and Ermengarde of Brittany is a boon for our understanding. Here at last, Robert expresses himself personally and at a moment of decisive development. Confronted by critics and, even more powerfully, the ardor of a disciple, Robert needed to appear wise. His reassurance in the form of founding Fontevraud shows that he sensed the need for concessions. Renaud of Martigné had scolded him for not sending wives back to angry husbands. In a role reversal, Robert returned Ermengarde to Count Alan while Geoffrey of Vendôme denounced her for having given up the austere life of the cloister. Marbode had condemned the vagabond's extreme asceticism; now Robert preached moderation in all things and exalted the established order. The criticism of the cathedral schoolmaster to which Robert must have

41. Ps 105/106:3; Mt 5:6; Mt 5:10.
42. Lk 6:22; Jn 15:18; Mt 10:25.
43. Prv 3:12 and Heb 12:6; Jb 5:17; Rv 3:19.

been sensitive was Marbode's suspicion of hypocrisy spread over an ostentatious humility. Debasement wore gold and purple while the martyr remained secret.

But fundamentally, the old hermit renounced nothing. He had channeled the raging flood that had always borne him, made it quieter and put it underground, but it was as powerful as ever. Beneath a cheerful exterior, he rejoiced in the insults, exulting in his Lord's blows and men's disapproval. What did Robert really think when reading in turn the warnings from Marbode and Geoffrey—that he had fallen into error or that he was the chosen of God? The peacefulness that the master proposed to Ermengarde is very strained, poisoned with the pleasure of an upside-down triumph. On one point alone did Robert give himself up to his heart's desire, without stiffening, without guile (yet with, perhaps, the prosaic hope of gaining alms for himself). His real mission, as in Rouen, is of mercy:

Be merciful to all the poor, but still more toward the destitute and most of all to the servants of faith who have left the world for God. Hear the Lord saying: "Blessed are the merciful, for they shall obtain mercy." And again: "Be merciful just as your Father is merciful, He who makes His sun rise above the good and the wicked, and makes it rain on the just and the unjust." And elsewhere Scripture says: "He apportioned and gave to the poor, and His justice abides forever." It does not say He gave to the rich, but to the poor. "Alms free man from death" and do not allow him to fall into darkness. . . .[44]

BERTRADE

After the death of Ermengarde's mother, three women in succession were welcomed into and removed from Fulk le Réchin's bed. Then came Bertrade of Montfort. In 1092, she left Fulk of her own accord to join King Philip I of France. Georges Duby recount-

44. Gal 6:10; Mt 5:7; Lk 6:36; Mt 5:45; Ps 111/112:9; Tb 4:11.

ed the conflict over this union, revealing its deep workings.[45] The motivation for each party was exactly the opposite of what might be expected. On three occasions, the Church condemned the king with its harshest punishment: excommunication. In October 1094, the papal legate Hugh of Die and thirty-two archbishops gathered at Autun hurled the first anathema. A year later, at Clermont, Pope Urban II took the trouble to renew the sentence personally while occupied with his impressive crusading project. When the king insisted on keeping Bertrade, he was excluded from the community of the faithful for the third time by papal legates at a council in Poitiers in 1100. According to Ivo of Chartres, who was present at the Clermont meeting and is therefore the best witness, the couple was condemned not for adultery or bigamy but for incest. To be exact, the problem was kinship in the seventh degree—between the king and Bertrade's husband.[46]

Philip's stubbornness is no less surprising. For a king—an anointed lord, pastor of the realm, peer of bishops—to live in sin and have fingers pointed at him was a disability hard to bear. Scarcely did he enter a city before prayer services ceased and church bells fell silent. A story tells that one day, Bertrade ordered church doors broken down so Mass could be celebrated there by compliant priests. Use of force and rage show the deep wound the ecclesiastical curse made. To withstand this challenge, the king needed to be assured he was well within his rights, certain of having made a legitimate marriage to the daughter of the lord of Montfort. Georges Duby saw in this matter the expression of a moral model of dynastic interests, opposed to the clerical model. The king's first wife, Bertha of Frisia, had given him only one puny son, and that after nine years. Bertrade had given proof of fertility

---

45. For what follows, see Duby, *The Knight, the Lady, and the Priest*, esp. 3–18.

46. Incest prohibitions encompassed both blood and marriage, and thus Bertrade, as the wife of Philip's distant cousin Fulk, could not marry him.

in the bed of Fulk le Réchin. She assured the king of a fine group of heirs, three children, two of them boys. Her first husband, moreover, found nothing to complain about initially. It took a papal legate to shake up and provoke the count of Anjou, then the meddling of the pope himself—at the stop in Angers in February of 1096 when he urged Robert to preach—for Fulk at last to vent his rage (and think of something other than finding multiple substitutes for Bertrade). The indignation was short-lived. In 1106, the supposed rivals, king and count, shared a banquet table, Bertrade having the place of honor between the two cousins.

If the men's thoughts are hard to read, Bertrade's are impenetrable. What did she think about either of her husbands? How did she feel about the curses reforming clerics hurled at her? Despite definite and repeated promises to the contrary by the royal couple, they remained together until Philip's death in 1108. Fulk died the next year. Bertrade returned to Angers and the side of her son, Count Fulk V; it was around this time that the young count's half-sister Ermengarde received the letter from Robert. Following in the footsteps of their vassals of Montsoreau and the vicinity, the counts of Anjou took Fontevraud under their protection. Each visit by the count to the budding institution was the occasion for generous gifts. Surviving charters show that Fulk the Younger and his mother came to offer bounty to their client foundation at least four times. There is no evidence that Bertrade ever gave herself over to penance, instead appearing in all her splendor, as adored mother of the count and, even more, as the queen she never ceased to be.

In 1114, Bertrade took the veil at Fontevraud. Here, too, she behaved royally. She went with an entourage: her sister Isabelle, countess of Conches-Toesny, her nieces Jeanne Payenne and Denise of Montfort. She went with property: the land of Hautes-Bruyères, a few miles from the fortress of the lords of Montfort, donated with the permission of her stepson, King Louis VI, on which site a priory of Fontevraud was established. Bertrade settled there and died soon afterwards. Was the chronicler William of Malmesbury right to believe that "this woman's delicate body could not bear the toil of religious life"?[47] Or did she enter only near death? At the approach of death, which people of this period appear never to have mistaken, she was finally stricken with remorse for having defied the prohibitions of the Church, just as the time of her judgment drew near.

Robert attached great importance to his fleeting disciple. At Christmas in 1115, by which time he no longer felt at all healthy, he went to make sure that all was in order at Hautes-Bruyères, passing the Feast of the Nativity in the company of the newly installed nuns. Once before, a long time ago, he had played a part in Bertrade's story. Did she know? It was at the Council of Poitiers in 1100, where King Philip got his third warning. Geoffrey the Fat, the hagiographer of Bernard of Tiron, remembered it this way:

> At this time, the cardinals John and Benedict, legates of the Apostolic See, called a council at Poitiers. One hundred forty prelates responded to the appeal and struck Philip, the king of France, with anathema because of the wife of Count Fulk of Anjou, whom the king kept adulterously. Present at the proclamation of this excommunication was Duke William of Aquitaine. This enemy of all modesty and holiness, fearing the same punishment for similar sins and enflamed with rage, ordered that the whole company be robbed, beaten, and killed. When his servants began to carry out the command, bishops and abbots ran off in every direction, seeking safe hiding-places to save their lives. But Bernard and Robert of Arbrissel, who were present at the council, very courageous defenders of justice and enemies of every iniquity and injustice, stood their ground when all the others fled shamefully. They steadfastly refused to renounce undertaking the excommunication, judging it most glorious to suffer death and insults for Christ. Although their persecutors did not put them to death, the two had suffered martyrdom of a sort.[48]

47. William of Malmesbury, *Gesta Regum Anglorum* 1: 732–733 (section 404).

48. Geoffrey the Fat, *Life of Bernard*, section 48 (Beck, *Saint Bernard de Tiron*, 364–365; PL 172: 1396).

This text is interesting for more than one reason. In this late version, written in the 1140s, the accusation of adultery has been substituted for the sin of consanguinity, this substitution a sign of the normalizing of marriage according to clerical morality. William of Aquitaine could have had two motivations, not mutually exclusive, for intruding. Like Philip, he lived in what reformers called concubinage, and doubtless, as the author suggests, solidarity among males put out of their ease played a part. At a deeper level, the king was his lord, and in a vassal's eyes, Philip had not offended the code of their caste with this second, fertile union—rather the contrary. As for Robert and Bernard, the hagiographer gives them a place of honor. In a time when martyrdom had become a faraway dream, what an opportunity for these divine athletes to be able to show their determination to experience it! Jean-Marc Bienvenu supposed, not without reason, that the two friends were at the council not as deliberating members, but had instead been summoned to give an account of the exact status of the troops they led.[49] Fontevraud had not yet been founded; this was the era of Marbode's criticisms. By their courageous stance, committing themselves resolutely to the service of reform as desired at the highest levels, the two suspects perhaps were trying to earn the leniency of their judges.

Comparing these two scenes, fifteen years apart, illuminates Robert's exact place in this moral crisis rocking the West. The sources themselves impose discontinuity: there is Robert, beaten and kicked, defying authority to condemn Philip and his wife, then Robert welcoming into his order the same Bertrade, when both she and Robert were nearing the end of their lives, and showing great care for one another. In the conflict of the two marriage models, the former parish priest of Arbrissel was on the side of clerics and reform, so very sure he was fighting the good fight that some of its

49. Bienvenu, *L'étonnant fondateur de Fontevraud,* 71–73.

first blows fell on him. Such was Robert's charisma that, having condemned, he offered asylum, appeal, and mercy. An epitaph attributed (without evidence) to the poet Hildebert of Lavardin, bishop of Le Mans, says of the founder of Fontevraud that he took care "to root out sin, not sinners."[50] Chance praise? Perhaps, this time, we should read the source literally.

THE WOMEN OF MENAT

This series of encounters will end as it began, with an anonymous document removed from its context, a "miracle." I think it is by the same author as the second *vita* of Robert of Arbrissel, in which case it could be attributed without doubt to Brother Andreas. Whoever took the trouble to record it did not fail to understand its significance.

One day when Robert was in Auvergne, he came to a place called Menelay l'Abbaye, armed with the fervor of faith, to preach in this monastery. The people of the country told him that women could not go in the church, and if any one of them presumed to enter, she would die at once. Learning this, the Lord's good servant, since he wanted to go and preach, led in several women against the will of those who stood watch at the doors, and showed them before all present that their lies were impious. Then the doorkeepers began devoutly to beg St. Meneleus and to cry aloud that it should please him to take vengeance on such presumption, scorn, and insult. Rich in spirit and discernment, the holy man replied, "Alas, simple people, do not continue such foolish prayers in vain! Know instead that the saints are not the enemies of the brides of Jesus Christ. For what you are saying is absurd and the purity of the catholic faith clearly says the opposite—as it is written in the Gospel concerning the blessed sinful woman who kissed the feet of the Redeemer, washed them with her tears, dried them with her hair, and

---

50. The poem is printed in PL 171: 1391–1392; translation in Venarde, *Robert of Arbrissel*, 114.

poured ointment on His very worthy head.[51] And so who dares to say that there should be any church into which a woman is not permitted entry, if she is not forbidden by reason of faults and sins? Which is the greater thing, God's material temple or the spiritual temple in which God lives? If a woman takes and eats the body and blood of Jesus Christ, think what folly it is to believe that she may not enter a church." After he had shown the truth, this wrong ceased and totally perished.[52]

This miracle is a fight in which the stakes are womankind, a clash between the itinerant troupe and the local people, a battle of the saints between Robert and Meneleus, and, most importantly of all, a conflict of cultures, those of an enlightened cleric and popular religion. The sides are unequal, for it is truth versus error. Like women, "the people" here are mute, crushed in the story and by the telling of it, reduced at its mercy to nothing but silence. What, then, was this tradition that banned women from entering a church? It requires an archeologist's patience to uncover the prehistory and guess at its meaning.

The Menelay l'Abbaye of the story is the monastery of Menat in Auvergne. Since at least the ninth century, relics said to be those of St. Meneleus were venerated there. The cult aroused interest in knowing more about the saint. Around his bones grew up a legend. In the tenth or eleventh century, a *vita* of Meneleus was written down.[53] It tells us that Meneleus lived in the seventh century. An extreme distrust of women comes through in this apocryphal and fantastic account. Meneleus, born in Anjou, was of very noble birth, as was necessarily the case for every early medieval saint. His father wanted him to marry the daughter of Lord Barontus, but the teenage son had secretly made a vow of chastity earlier, at age sev-

---

51. Lk 7:36–38.

52. This anecdote, at the end of late medieval French version of Andreas's *vita*, was first published in Dalarun, *L'impossible sainteté*, 297–298. The original edition of the present book duplicated the Middle French language.

53. Latin *vita* in AASS, July, volume 5, 308–319.

en. He ran away from his wife after a few days. In the solitary valley of Menat in Auvergne where he had taken refuge, Meneleus
met Theofrid, a monk from the abbey of Chaumillac, who took
Meneleus off to his monastery to educate him. Seven years later, at
the command of an angel, Meneleus set out again for Menat. His
mother, sister, and in-name-only wife arrived there after searching
for him far and wide. Another angel appeared, this one giving the
command to settle the women well away from him. The next to ar-
rive was Barontus, furious, appearing suddenly on the trail of the
fugitive women. He drew his sword to kill Meneleus, but went
blind, his hands knotted up. The saint, of course, cured Barontus,
and forgave him in exchange for numerous properties. Continuing
in the eventful mode, the end of the *vita* tells of the abuses show-
ered on Meneleus by Queen Brunhilde. Even in this misogynist account, nothing can justify the prohibition Robert of Arbrissel came
across in the twelfth century.

The trail would come to a sudden end were it not for the name
of Theofrid. Restorer of the ancient monastery of Chaumillac, he
left it his name, popularized: Saint-Chaffre de Monastier, south of
Le Puy-en-Velay. The *Life of Theofrid*, which has him dying in 732
as a martyr to Saracens, merits no more trust than the account of
his disciple; it would appear, in fact, as if the legend of Meneleus inspired one about his master and that the Theofrid *vita* came even
later.[54] One passage is especially interesting. Newly elected as abbot of Chaumillac, Theofrid took a series of steps to ensure the
good order of his monastery, in particular seeing to it that nothing
would trouble the calm of the sanctuary. "Women who wanted to
enter had a place far off, around the door of the temple. And although some do not take into account the purpose of the obser-
vance and think it was a divine prohibition of long ago, the practice

---

54. Latin *vita* in AASS, October, volume 8, 527–533. The passage quoted in
this paragraph is at ibid., 529 (section 14).

will remain unchanged forever." This is exactly the prohibition Robert came up against several centuries later. Here is the trail, then, but the meaning of the practice remains obscure.

A return to the literal point of departure, Menat, points in another direction, since the *Life of Meneleus* is not the oldest text concerning this monastery. Menat is mentioned in the earlier *vita* of St. Calais.[55] Composed in the Carolingian period and circulated in two slightly different versions, this Life claims to give an account of facts of the Merovingian era.[56] From what is apparently an historically worthless account come a few tidbits very useful for understanding Robert's actions at Menat. Calais was a native of Auvergne and was a young monk at Menat. Leaving to respond to the call of the desert, he ended up founding a monastery that bears his name, Saint-Calais in Maine. Shortly before his death, Calais submitted to a very awkward request. Queen Ultrogode, wife of his benefactor Childebert, son of Clovis, sent messengers to ask that she be allowed to come see him.[57] Calais, realizing the danger that such a visit would pose, refused this favor and decreed that thereafter his monastery would be off limits to women—a rule, the text says, that has been respected, with God's help, to this day. So it was effectively the work of the Almighty that the custom remained inviolate, as revealed in one of the posthumous miracles of St. Calais. A woman named Gunda wanted badly to defy the prohibition. She disguised herself as a man to elude the monks' surveillance and enter the sanctuary where the saint's body lay buried. As she entered,

55. Latin *vita* in AASS, July, volume 1, 90–99. The saint's Latin name is Carilefus. The incidents discussed in this paragraph are at ibid., 96–97 (sections 27–29: Ultrogode) and 98 (sections 34–36: Gunda).

56. "Carolingian" refers to the family of Charlemagne and is shorthand for the eighth and ninth centuries in Western Europe; the predecessor dynasty, from the early sixth to early eighth century, was the Merovingian.

57. The names of Ultrogode and Childebert place the story in the mid-sixth century.

though, a terrible punishment befell her. Here is the heart of the matter.

The Ultrogode and Gunda anecdotes allow some understanding of the custom of prohibition in Auvergne and Maine inasmuch as the two versions of the *Life of Calais* vary in some meaningful ways. Although the two versions recount more or less the same facts, the styles are very different. The first version is cruder and shorter; its author says he has collected the stories from local people. A Latin-literate writer would almost certainly have been a cleric, but this author was a man of little refinement who echoed popular traditions passed down orally for generations without batting an eye. The second version reshaped an all-too crude narrative, embellishing, refining, and embroidering it. The second hagiographer was an accomplished scholar who tried to carve sophistication into the raw material.[58]

Why did the ascetic Calais fear to allow the queen access to his monastery? In the first version, he refused to receive her "in fear that his disciples' spirits would be disturbed in some way" and he limits himself to decree that "in the future, the female sex will not have access to the monastery's enclosure."[59] In the second version, Calais begins by asking himself, "How is it that the queen so wants to see me . . . made hideous by the filth of fasting? I know, for certain I know the intense heat of the old Enemy, with which, in the soft sweetness of paradise, he broke down man's might through the weakness of woman. I must be on guard against a woman's look lest I be taken in by the Devil's snares, living as I do here in the harsh desert, when one who rejoiced in a life of pleasure in paradise and even the company of God was still seduced by evil per-

---

58. The earlier version is printed in *Monumenta Germaniae Historica, Scriptorum Rerum Merovingicarum* (Hannover, 1885–), 3: 386–394. See below, note 64, for a different edition.

59. Ibid., 393 (section 11).

suasion." He replies to the queen's envoys, "As long as I am flesh
and blood, I will not see a woman's face and this monastery that I
built with God's help will never offer a woman entry. It is not fitting for us considered to be Christ's household to sell the sight of
ourselves to women."[60]

From one version to the other, the play of looks on the body of
the opposite sex, the play of desire, takes on added intensity. There
is an important role reversal: in the first version, the temptation
lies in the hearts of the brothers, but in the revision, the woman,
the serpent's agent, becomes the promoter of sin. Differing in degree of misogyny, the two versions both draw from the same literary source—once again, the Lives of the desert fathers. It is hardly
surprising to find here, again, the "matter of Egypt." Before the end
of the fourth century, this material, written and oral, had reached
Sulpicius Severus, the hagiographer of St. Martin of Tours. The
Life of Martin was the first text by which the West found out about
the challenge of Eastern asceticism, which retained its allure
through the Middle Ages and beyond.[61] In the seventeenth century,
the solitaries of Port-Royal immersed themselves in the *Lives of the
Fathers* translated by Arnauld d'Andilly.[62] Here is the legend of St.

60. AASS, July, volume 1, 97 (section 28).

61. Sulpicius Severus, "Life of Martin of Tours," in *Early Christian Lives*, trans.
White, 129–159.

62. The *Vitae patrum*, meaning "Lives of the Fathers," is the name for a massive collection of anecdotes about the monks of Egypt popular in the Middle Ages
(PL 73–74; see next note). Port-Royal was a wealthy French nunnery that moved
in the early seventeenth century from outside Paris into the city. One of its abbesses in the seventeenth century, Marie Angélique de Sainte Madeleine Arnauld, came
under the influence of Jansenism, a strain of Catholic thought named after Bishop
Cornelius Jansen (1585–1638), author of several theological works espousing
moralism aimed at a return to the primitive Church and challenging papal infalli-
bility. In the first half of the seventeenth century, the former site of the abbey, referred to as Port-Royal-des-Champs, became a center for Jansenist adherents who
sometimes lived like hermits and were known as the solitaries of Port-Royal.
Abbess Angélique's brother Antoine Arnauld lived for some years at Port-Royal,

Calais that his hagiographers pieced together from sayings of the desert fathers.

In one story an old Roman matron went in devotion to see Abbot Arsenius. The abbot had been asked by Archbishop Theophilus to let her see him, but he had not consented. Therefore this lady went to the abbot's little cell. Finding him in front of the door, she threw herself at his feet. The extremely indignant abbot lifted her up and said, "If you want to see my face, then look." The lady, confused and frightened, did not look at the old man who said, "How did a woman like you dare to undertake such a long trip? You'll go back to Rome and tell other women you have seen Abbot Arsenius, and then they, too, will come to see me." She replied, "If God wishes me to return to Rome, I will not let any woman come here; I ask only that you pray for me and remember me always." "I will pray to God," answered the saint, "that he erase the memory of you from my heart." Hearing these words, the flustered woman went back to town and fell ill. The archbishop went to comfort her, but she said that she was dying of grief. The archbishop replied, "Don't you know that you are a woman and that it is through women that the Enemy attacks saints? That is why the old man said that to you, but he prays ceaselessly for your soul." She took comfort in these words and went back to Rome. Another anecdote tells that a brother had to carry his aged mother across a river, and covered his hands with his cloak. His mother asked him, "Why, son, did you cover your hands?" He answered, "Because a woman's body is a fire, and if I touched you the memory of other women might come into my soul."[63]

---

teaching and writing textbooks. Another brother, the poet Robert Arnauld d'Andilly, translated the *Vitae patrum* into French for the community there. The scholars of Port-Royal-des-Champs stubbornly ignored royal and papal orders to give up the heresy of Jansenism and the community was suppressed in 1704.

63. These two stories come from a part of the *Vitae patrum* known as the *Verba seniorum*, literally "old men's words." For full translations of each episode, see Bene-

This last episode links Calais to Meneleus. It was in the same spirit that Meneleus isolated his mother, sister, and wife from the men's monastery. Whether in Egypt, Auvergne, or Maine, these utterly harsh stories, so severe that they grate on us today, all had the same goal: to strengthen the claustration Western monasticism implemented through the example of Eastern austerities from the early Middle Ages. Accustomed to some men making the choice of such an imprisonment, we should try to imagine how very unnatural it must have seemed at the beginning. It took a violent approach to impose it on the men inside and the others outside the cloister, hence the harshness and arrogance of the stories. The legend of St. Calais thus preserved the memory of the first time the prohibition was made in this part of Maine and proclaimed it at the expense of a queen to make it easier to remember. The tradition persisting centuries later attests to the success of the undertaking.

This new law, even if lived by only a small number of chosen people, nonetheless confronted and broke down an equilibrium apparently founded on the law of nature, according to which men and women lived together and procreated together. The Gunda anecdote, amidst a torrent of images, tried to integrate this foreign teaching and establish a new order of things. Here is the first version, which the hagiographer asserts everyone in the region knew:

A woman named Gunda, whom the secret Enemy had seduced, wanted to mock the Holy Spirit. She put on man's clothes and tried hard to enter the monastery of the blessed Calais to test the prediction he had made that nobody of the female sex would ever be given the power to go in there. But by a just judgment of God, the moment she saw the closed entrance of the monastery, she was stricken by the Devil, thrown backward, and abused by him in a way so hateful that I am ashamed to tell it. He thrust her head between her thighs, acting this way so that she who had tried to press her impostor's kisses on sacred spaces, would be

dicta Ward, *The Desert Fathers: Sayings of the Early Christian Monks* (London, 2003), 9–10 (Arsenius and the Roman matron), 31 (the monk and his mother).

forced, shamefully bent over, to kiss the filthiest parts of her body. Thus a woman who had wanted to dress like a man would have to show her sex openly to anyone who wanted to see it. This happened so that women would never dare gather in this place and to make it clear that the prediction of the blessed Calais was true.[64]

Here was a popular reinterpretation of a monastic prohibition, toppling into the universe of magic.

Numerous legends of various civilizations grew up around these themes of breaking taboos of transvestitism and the invisible barrier around sacred space. More importantly, faced with the enigmatic prohibition of the monks, the villagers found their response, their answer: the suspicion of guilt concerning relations between the sexes by the monks' stubborn chastity was totally focused on a woman. Her twisted body was ridiculed and her punishment was to expose her sex. The penalty is laughter, the throaty laughter of farce and womanizing—male jokes at the expense of the inferior sex scorned as a weaker sex. Punishments of this kind appear in many legends, but never with such daring. A violent wind, for example, lifts the skirts of women who wanted to enter a saint's sanctuary. Laughter averts fear and as always in folkloric culture, ambivalence rules, here the fear of defilement, of a woman who has just become debauched dancing or stripping down in sacred places. In this village in Maine, the community made the first move. What might be a willful gesture of provocation becomes a penalty suffered; a challenge mutates into a punishment. In both cases, the crowd assembles as voyeurs.

The slap was too rough. The mud slung at the woman spattered those who slung it. "I am ashamed to tell it," says the hagiographer. A rewrite was called for. Here is Gunda again before the relics:

---

64. *Vita prima sancti Carilefi* (section 17) in Laurentius Surius, *De probatis sanctorum historiis*, 7 vols. (Cologne, 1576–1586), 7: 39.

When she sought entry to the interior of the sanctuary and wanted avidly to see it, her eyes were struck by a sudden flash and she who had so irreverently wanted to contemplate the forbidden now lost the right to see ordinary things. At the same time, she was entered by a demon and a stream of black blood flowed from a hole in her chest. She wet the ground around her with a free-flowing stream of blood.[65]

In this second version, the female body is not ridiculed but polluted. The mysterious stream of blood that wets the ground doubtless elevates menstrual blood into a punishment from heaven, the dark side of fertility. The prohibition of Calais, drawn from the literary tradition of the desert fathers to bolster the basic tenets of monasticism and reinterpreted in grotesque mode by popular tradition, finds here its ultimate, mythical rewriting and resonates with the curse of Eve.

Around 1114, Robert of Arbrissel approached Menat. A little village clung to the green left side of the Sioule River valley around the monastery, taken over by monks from Cluny, becoming a Cluniac house, in 1107. The old taboo that had expanded to include Saint-Chaffre and Saint-Calais was also preserved here, more than half a millennium later. Nothing had changed; women did not have the right to enter the church. Now the penalty was simple and radical: death. So where did the women of Menat go to Mass? Did the ban have the ludicrous effect of exempting them from it? The chapel built for the women of Meneleus's family was out of the way, a little too far for these parishioners to go. In the center of the village is a dilapidated old Romanesque church, defaced, restored contrary to reason and yet somehow still beautiful. It has still today a striking feature: a disproportionately large porch, built in the thirteenth century but redone according to an older plan. The *Life of Theofrid* explains the enigma: the women would have gathered around the door; the vast porch would shelter them while they re-

---

65. AASS, July, volume 1, 98 (section 35).

mained on the threshold, outside the forbidden sanctuary. A miracle concerning St. Stephen of Obazine shows that at his foundation on the western slopes of the Massif Central, the same taboo was current in the middle of the twelfth century.[66] At Menat, everyone was united in the custom. The inhabitants, the villagers, announced the ban to Robert's troop. The porters, doubtless monks, called for the saint's vengeance. Cluniac rigor concerning cloistering adapted well to folkloric legend. From Ultrogode to Gunda, a sacred union of monastic and popular traditions had been remade. Robert of Arbrissel was dealing with a united front.

His first act of defiance should have sufficed to assure victory. He had women go in with him and they did not die. However, the success of this ordeal did not weaken the superstitious in the slightest, so fixed was the idea in their skulls. Then Robert spoke and the Word triumphed where an act had not. His remarks were simple, clear, and illustrated with examples and references that everybody could understand. He willingly asked questions, as if he wanted to give his listeners the means to convince themselves rather than stun them with his own convictions. It was a little crude, doubtless, but already arms were reaching out to harm him. "Alas, simple people, do not continue such foolish prayers in vain!" Robert contrasted "the purity of the catholic faith" to the local tradition that the hagiographer called "impious lies." The tradition in which *he* placed himself was the Gospel. The woman who opened the way of salvation to women was Mary Magdalene, "the blessed sinful woman who kissed the feet of the Redeemer, washed them with her tears, dried them with her hair, and poured ointment on His very worthy head."

This praise of caresses was not necessarily a self-interested plea. The master of Fontevraud, late in life, was well beyond the

---

66. *Vie de saint Etienne d'Obazine*, ed. and trans. Michel Aubrun (Clermont-Ferrand, 1970), 240–241 (Book III, section 31; Latin text and French translation).

extraordinary punishments of which Marbode and Geoffrey had accused him, as this sentence bears eloquent witness: "And so who dares to say that there should be any church into which a woman is not permitted entry, if she is not forbidden by reason of faults and sins?" By recognizing personal responsibility in the face of sin, Robert demolished the idea of "femininity" as "evil female essence." In placing women under the patronage of the Magdalene, he saved them from sin twice. First, nobody is a sinner except when she sins, and even then she has the mercy of Christ, come to save sinners.

Robert recognized women as having a consciousness. Even so, he realized that there was a heavy burden to relieve, the image of the body fiercely persisting in the old legend. "Which is the greater thing, God's material temple or the spiritual temple in which God lives? If a woman takes and eats the body and blood of Jesus Christ, think what folly it is to believe that she may not enter a church." The taboo was swept away with the back of the hand. Woman's body is sacred, a temple of the Holy Spirit, tabernacle of the Eucharist. This makes a complete circle from Bethany to the Lord's Supper. The woman who "takes and eats the body and blood of Jesus Christ" is, like the blessed sinner, promised redemption. The Eucharist thus celebrates union with the body of Christ at Bethany. Sharp divisions between consciousness and flesh, men and women, broke down. The dawn of a new idea has arrived, one already self-assured in its bold youth, an idea of the individual and her dignity. In his way, Robert renewed the ancient idea that salvation came into the world through a woman and took bodily form in her.

A paradox of the mental universe of the Middle Ages is that all currents that followed, crossed, and confronted one another, constellations of ideas and images we would call ideologies, drew their materials solely from Scripture and tradition. The two images of women that collided at Menat came from the same source, the desert fathers. Even in Egyptian spirituality, headlong flight from

women and the test of the shared bed both came from the same ascetic impulse and are but two successive stages of it: after the training that made desire disappear came hand-to-hand combat, proof
after the trial. Robert broke his body in the desert of Craon, just
like Calais and Meneleus in their solitudes, before going to face the
fire of the flesh. It was then that he reached new spiritual territory.

The two miracles of Rouen and Menat authenticate one another in that the same spirit animated both, against the tide of most
contemporary discourse. While the post-Gregorian Church used
everything that Scripture and tradition could offer in the attempt
to make the clergy like monks and remove them from the temptress, woman, thereby rather oddly finding an echo in the obscurity
of folkloric culture, Robert by contrast delivered women from the
two opposite images of femininity, Eve and Mary. Contrary to what
is usually said, reference to the Virgin crushes real-world women
more than it elevates them. Defeated in advance by comparison to
the virginal fertility of Mary, women sink to the rank of Eve, the
temptress, the agent of the serpent, the polluted one. To counter
biblical images, Robert referred to the Bible. At Rouen and Menat,
the model was neither Eve nor Mary, but the infinite, fluid, living
composite of the Magdalene. From Robert's point of view, faces
everywhere lifted like the dawn.

5

THE SEVENTH DEGREE
OF HUMILITY

CHOOSING HUMILIATION

Many years passed as Robert preached, converted, and founded new communities at Beaugency, Redon, Rouen, Angers, Bourges, Menat, Agen, and Toulouse. The wandering apostle did not take good care of himself. "'Robert' means 'strong as an oak,'" explains his hagiographer.[1] Finally, though, his strength deserted him and he felt it. In the summer of 1115, he was quite elderly, seventy or more. What was wrong with him, exactly? Nobody knew and nobody worried much about it, noting only that "new ailments were added to old ones"—fevers, disabilities. That is what mattered. In the account of Brother Andreas that will now guide us step-by-step through the master's last six months—an account that draws its whole rhythm from the progress of illness, its attacks, remissions, and pain—there is no question of anything more specific than incapacity. Robert could literally no longer stand and therefore called together the brothers of Fontevraud from his bed. "Behold, my dearest sons whom I begot in the Gospel: I am hard pressed by illness and enter on the way of all flesh."

Death was there and he knew it. He announces it, very calmly and ceremonially, no fewer than eight times in the account that fol-

---

1. Andreas, *Second Life*, section 2 (PL 1062: 1058).

lows. In this era, death was neither hidden nor sad, but it was solemn. The dying man had to make arrangements to pass on power and property, if heaven had granted any, for the salvation of his soul and in the interest of those who would survive him. In this case, the inheritance was immense. The wealth of Fontevraud had ballooned: land, forests, vineyards, mills, innumerable gifts, and more than twenty priories spread across the whole west of France. At this point, Robert thought above all about things left to do.

"Ask yourselves, while I am still alive, if you want to persevere in your purpose, that is, to obey Christ's handmaids for the salvation of your souls. For you know that everything I have built everywhere, with God's help, I have submitted to their power and dominion. But if you do not wish to stay with them as you began, I give you freedom to choose another religious order with my advice."

"Far be it from us, dearest father, that we ever abandon them, for as you know, we can do no better elsewhere! Far be it that we abandon your undertaking! Before God and the saints, and in your hands, we all unanimously and freely promise stability and perseverance in the Church of Fontevraud."[2]

Their apparent enthusiasm should not deceive us. This dialogue from the summer of 1115 that opens the second *vita* offers a clear refutation of those who think of Robert as a troubadour and believe, along with Jules Michelet, that at his foundation there presided "the idea of making a woman the queen of monasteries and living under her in pleasurable obedience, a mixture of love and holiness."[3] In the first place, that the exchange happened at all is telling. The master, sensing his death approaching, thought it of the utmost importance to have the brothers renew their vow of submission. It did not go without saying. Some must have thought about leaving the order and Robert's concluding remark shows the extent of their determi-

---

2. Andreas, *Second Life*, section 3 (PL 162: 1058–1059; Venarde, *Robert of Arbrissel*, 26–27).

3. Michelet, *Œuvres complètes* 4: 341.

nation: he preferred to relieve them of their vows instead of impos-
ing a yoke that would chafe sooner or later. Very discreetly, the hagiographer notes that "nearly all" made the moving reply just quoted, which is to say that a small number of them took advantage of
the authorization to seek their salvation elsewhere.

Urgency increased as the fever burned a little hotter every day.
Robert sent messengers to neighboring dioceses, asking bishops
and abbots to come have a council by his side.[4] They gathered in
September. "I sense that my end is near and that is why I sent for
you, so that with your advice I could arrange the election of an
abbess for the benefit of our Church." They conceded that "it is
rather your advice that should be heeded, very dear father, for we
know for certain that more than any other mortal of our time, your
advice carries weight. God gave you to the world as a guide of
souls." Sweet revenge for a vagabond against whom prelates had
thundered fifteen years earlier! He called them and they came run-
ning. The pious protector of the order, Peter of Poitiers, was not in
their number. He had died the year before from the ill treatment of
William of Aquitaine, but his church, still without a bishop, had
sent its officials. In the face of the devastation of neighboring dioceses, Robert's teaching only had more prestige. From his bed, he
dominated the assembled company. Still, he needed them, less for
their advice than their presence and their support—and so that
they would note what he said. "You know, my very dear ones, that
everything I created in the world, I did for the good of our
nuns. . . . What is more, I submitted both myself and my disciples
to their service for the salvation of our souls." Nearly word for
word he went over the discussion he had already had with the
brothers and explained its consequences; it now remained to ap-
point an abbess. It was quite clever of the founder to present these

4. The council of churchmen and the election of Petronilla as abbess discussed
in the next several paragraphs are recounted in Andreas, *Second Life*, sections 4–9
(PL 162: 1059–1062; Venarde, *Robert of Arbrissel*, 27–31).

eccentricities as a foregone conclusion. "So I ask you: am I permitted to name a lay convert abbess? For I know that the dignity of the position calls for a virgin—I know it." There follows a strange discussion. At some length, Robert criticizes young women raised in the cloister, incapable of managing the affairs of the order, who know how to do nothing but sing psalms. These foolish women would ruin Fontevraud. "That is why I do not want to entrust this office to any cloister virgin, for fear of seeming to destroy what I have built." He will give it, on the contrary, to a wise woman, a good manager who has come up against the world.

Such a decision was a sign of the times. The perfectly closed and virginal world of the monastery, focused entirely on the celestial Jerusalem of which it was an earthly reflection, did not match the religious spirit of the early twelfth century. The prestige of Cluny, where processions went on to infinity, where Mass succeeded Mass to anticipate the chants of eternity, where young children given to the community, "oblates," were raised far from the stains of the world—the prestige was still great, but it was the respect owed to the phenomenal relic of another age. Cîteaux, founded three years before Fontevraud and in the same spirit of novelty, refused oblates, welcoming only hardened men and putting them to work. Yes, the Benedictine Rule told the Cluniacs to sanctify themselves through labor, but it was the work given to extensive reading, meditation, and never-ending prayer services. At Cîteaux, they rolled up their sleeves. Of course the "convert monks," crude peasants, worked the hardest, but the choir monks themselves, literate as they were, earned their pittance by the sweat of their brow—pittance and salvation, since the degradation still attached to manual labor was increased in value as penance.[5] So practice and its sym-

5. In Cistercian practice there were two different orders of monks, both the usual elite and literate community of the cloister and the *conversi*, peasants who voluntarily renounced the world and joined a monastery for life but whose social status and lack of education meant their work for God was focused on manual labor.

bolic meaning entwined and urged one another forward; by knocking into each other they went forward.

The general critique of foolish virgins that Robert made was not praise of wise women. "I continue to aspire to Mary in the heavens, but I choose Martha who knows how to manage worldly affairs wisely."[6] He did so with regret, for if the virgins were unfit, the women of experience were, in the end, unworthy. Finally, Robert reversed the terms of the choice. If the tabernacle is covered with goatskins, it is to protect the scarlet fabric that adorns the interior so that nothing can dull its brilliance. Virginity remains, certainly, the most precious of treasures and the future abbess, a conscientious administrator, will find herself at once lowered to the rank of a nanny's hide. One of the assembled clergy, an archpriest of the diocese of Angers, raised the bid: he had previously heard Pope Urban II confer abbacy on a matron who had had four husbands. These men knew how to make themselves understood in few words. The matter was settled. The assembly ended, having renewed its confidence in the venerable father of Fontevraud.

Everything had been said, but nothing done. It remained to designate the one to protect the community with her hide tanned by life. Robert alone would make this decision. He delayed and doubtless hesitated. He consulted further. A month passed, and at the end of October, he made his declaration: Petronilla of Chemillé would be abbess. "It seems fitting to me that one who bore along with me the labor of wandering and poverty should also bear the burden of comfort and prosperity." If it is good to bear poverty with the patience of Job (more than to seek it out), abundance of material goods is still the mark of divine favor, and even Christ's poor could glory in it. "Although she has been married, constrained

6. Lk 10:38–42. In this anecdote, Mary sat at Jesus' feet to listen to him speak while her sister Martha bustled around, busy with household cares.

by necessity I see nobody who would be more fitting for this high office." The least one could say is that Robert was not wild with enthusiasm for this faithful follower at the start. For his part, Baudri makes it clear that Petronilla would not have attained this honor if Hersende, the leader at the beginning, had still been alive.[7]

So why this choice? Hierarchies and kinship carried weight here. Robert appears to have been drawn to Hersende with a more instinctive confidence, but this first choice was linked to the ties of the widow to Gautier of Montsoreau, the castellan nearest to Fontevraud. Petronilla for her part was the first cousin of the influential Geoffrey of Vendôme. Does that mean Robert succumbed to pressure? There was some, doubtless, and Robert would have willingly paid attention to it. Concerned for the prosperity of the order, he knew that Petronilla could, at best, fit into aristocratic networks and present to the outside world a representative to be reckoned with. It was already more than enough that the representative was female. It was in this spirit that Robert took care to confirm the election of Petronilla with the papal legate Gerard of Angoulême, who, for still more security, obtained a written confirmation from Pope Pascal II. The very idea of subordinating men to women was not exempt from the need to keep social hierarchies. The brothers were obscure, usually not titled nobles, at most knights. The matrons and virgins came from the families of barons. In his surprising advancement of women, Robert in a sense yielded to the ways of his era. It was perhaps more about Petronilla herself, rather than the lady of Chemillé or the daughter of the lords of Craon, that Robert had reservations. The sequel did something to justify his doubts.

For the moment, the newly elected Petronilla made herself humble. As soon as they told her the news, she sought, above all, means to decline the responsibility. "She feared—not unreasonably,

---

7. Baudri, *First Life*, section 21 (PL 162: 1054; Venarde, *Robert of Arbrissel*, 18).

since there was really something to fear—to take on the immeasurable burden of such an honor. On one hand, as a wise woman she dreaded her own weakness; on the other, she considered the magnitude of the office. What else to say?" It was truly difficult to be more disagreeable. Petronilla's denials were quasi-ritualistic. One did not accept an honor, especially of the spiritual kind, without first declaring oneself unworthy of it. Robert's messengers had to return to their task, pray, and urge, only to be declined again until finally, unwillingly, Petronilla accepted. The Middle Ages overflowed with this sort of politesse, which we would think of as Eastern, and it lasted a long time in Europe—how many refusals and postponed departures does it take before the offer of a drink is accepted?

What is much less ordinary is the insistence with which Andreas underlines that Petronilla had ample reason to fear her weakness, *imbecillitas*. "She has many traits worthy of recounting that I could tell. But because I confess to being her son, although quite unworthy, I will keep silent for the moment, lest I am thought desirous of anointing her head with the oil of flattery." Some historians have seen Andreas as the abbess's fawning toady. Such a view requires a lot of imagination. After having clearly let it be known that she did not merit the honor given her, Andreas pauses a moment to say a few good things about Petronilla. Some courtier!

One last jab gives a sense of the events as they unfolded at Fontevraud. Andreas reports that in all the foundations of the order, the houses of women were placed under the patronage of Mary and the men's chapels were dedicated to St. John the Evangelist "so that the brothers would have an example of service to the brides of Christ." Here the hagiographer softens, reminding us of the touching scene on Calvary, Jesus in his last moment entrusting his tearful mother to the disciple he loved.[8] "I do not do this in order to

8. Jn 19:25–27.

compare our service to St. John's, knowing without a doubt that this excellent Virgin, seated next to her son in paradise, is without peer."[9] This is harsh: the brothers are indeed imitators of John, but the sisters are unworthy of Mary's patronage.

It is evident that the promotion of women to head the order is always linked, in the account of Andreas, to a reminder of their unworthiness. That, he thought, was the spirit of Fontevraud, a world turned upside-down. As a conqueror of the sexual ordeal, Robert sought in the very organization of his order a prolongation of his penance, the ultimate test, expiation of his first sin. In the Benedictine Rule, which the master knew well and altered for greater rigor in establishing a food and clothing regimen for his disciples, there is a description of the slow ascent through degrees of humility meant, like Jacob's ladder, to lead reliably to God. The climb to the seventh degree means humility become humiliation, when "not only does the monk declare with his mouth that he is the least and most worthless of all, but also believes this from the bottom of his heart and says with the prophet, 'I am a worm and not a man, the scorn of humanity and the people's refuse. I was exalted, then humbled and confounded.'"[10] Fontevraud, a mostly female monastery, was conceived as a matter of priority "for the salvation of the brothers" and it was to that end that the founder said he submitted them to the service of the sisters. It was a degrading service, for there is nothing more humiliating than obedience to a superior one secretly believes unworthy of the rank. Reward, however, would come from the humiliation as surely as the last would be first.

Where is the question of the *women's* salvation in all these dis-

9. Andreas, *Second Life*, section 11 (PL 162: 1063; Venarde, *Robert of Arbrissel*, 32).

10. The seventh chapter of Benedict's Rule is entitled "On Humility." See www.osb.org/rb. In a dream, the Hebrew patriarch Jacob saw a ladder to heaven on which angels ascended and descended (Gn 28:10–16). The quotations in the Rule are from Psalms 21/22:7 and 87/88:16.

cussions? It is elsewhere, at Rouen and Menat. On Calvary, John supported Mary, fainting in the majesty of her grief. Their mutual care, for a moment, weakened the intensity of their pain. On earth, another woman, her long hair spread out, had stayed on her knees at the Savior's feet since Bethany, and such is her rank: the lowest and the closest. Alone, nothing distracted her from the face that lit up her own.[11]

Robert's contemporary Stephen of Muret also founded an order that attracted attention. In his institution, the lay converts, rustics just off the farm, had authority over the choir monks, the learned clerics. This arrangement offered the priests of the order more leisure to devote themselves to contemplation (like the nuns of Fontevraud), and such absurd and praiseworthy submission was a surer path toward the heavenly home.[12] On the other hand, to *choose* a practice because it is "against nature" does not offer any real challenge to whatever is considered the natural order. In the organization of Fontevraud rested not the desire to promote women but the final avatar of agony, not a great mental revolution. It involved shifts, to be sure, but there remained in principle unanticipated consequences, perverse effects of asceticism like the elevation of laymen in Stephen of Muret's order and the valorization of work at Cîteaux. A matron served better to run the community because, like the cover for the tabernacle, she could weather storms "like a man."[13] This slip of Robert's puts things back in their place—or rather shows that they never really moved.

11. Lk 7:36–50. This woman, unnamed in the Gospel, was folded into the medieval composite of Mary Magdalene.

12. St. Stephen of Muret (1046–1124) was another hermit who attracted disciples in his native Auvergne. His followers established a community at Grandmont shortly after his death, the head of the small, austere order of Grandmontine hermits.

13. *Viriliter* is the adverb Robert uses, quoted by Andreas, *Second Life*, section 5 (PL 162: 1060).

THE LAST TOUR

The illness relaxed its grip for a while. The convalescent immediately seized the opportunity and left Fontevraud. We would
know of no single itinerary of this man who went back and forth so
much if Andreas had not taken care to record this journey, begun in
November 1115. It would be the last. Perhaps it was for that reason
that Robert hastened to go back on the road at the first sign of im-
provement, so he could see to the good order of far-flung houses
before death took him. Still, he dawdled, too. A dispute? He ran to
settle it. A friend in the area? He went to visit. Someone wanted to
hear him preach? He set off again. In these detours Robert's pleasure in travel is evident. It was a trait of medieval life to pass from
extreme stability to extreme mobility without any transition. People would spend many years within a small perimeter only to end
up on the road to Compostella or Jerusalem.[14] In a time when life
was so short, people knew better that they were here in passing, on
course, as they believed, for the Promised Land. They walked.
From mid-November to mid-February, Robert and his companions
covered over 400 miles: from Fontevraud to the Ile-de-France and
from there to the depths of Berry, not including detours—all this
for an aged man who by now agreed to go on horseback but who
had some trouble staying upright.

The first goal of this trip was to install some nuns—doubtless
Bertrade of Montfort and her relatives—at the priory of Hautes-
Bruyères.[15] These noble ladies were sent along ahead under the

14. Compostella, the Spanish resting place of Jesus' apostle St. James the
Greater, was along with Jerusalem and Rome the major pilgrimage destination for
European Christians in Robert of Arbrissel's time.

15. The journey that took Robert from Fontevraud to Hautes-Bruyères and
then to Orsan in the central French region of Berry, which is discussed on the next
several pages, is recounted in Andreas, *Second Life*, sections 12–22 (PL 162:
1063–1068; Venarde, *Robert of Arbrissel*, 32–38).

guidance of Petronilla. Robert followed just behind. He caught up to them on arrival at the Benedictine monastery of Saint-Florentin in Bonneval. The party stayed there and learned that Abbot Bernier was extremely angry at Bishop Ivo of Chartres. Robert was delighted to intervene. Again he left the nuns, now given over to the care of Prioress Angarde, as if he were not really of their company. He kept Petronilla with him and joined forces with his friend Bernard of Tiron, whose monastery was nearby. What was the nature of the quarrel between Bernier and Ivo? There are no details at all. What is certain is that Robert, arriving at Chartres, succeeded in reconciling the two estranged brother clerics.

Robert reached Hautes-Bruyères for Christmas. Among the buildings that remain there today, a church façade going to ruin still bears witness to the time when the round of prayer services gave rhythm to the lives of a handful of nuns. Robert inaugurated the newly founded priory and fittingly prepared for the celebration of the Nativity, "assiduous in fasting and prayers, insatiable in reading, spending whole nights in vigils, overflowing with tears, and admirable in teaching."

With Christmas barely over, the world took Robert back once more. The great Ivo of Chartres had just died and the designation of his successor was turning into civil war. The canons of the cathedral had led Geoffrey of Lèves to the episcopal throne through free election in the spirit of Gregorian reform. This was not to the taste of the powerful Count Thibaud IV, who had no intention of renouncing his traditional prerogatives and wanted to put forward his own candidate. When Robert got wind of the matter, negotiations had broken down, the good offices of Bernard of Tiron had served no purpose, and Chartres was in violent uproar. The count had ransacked the homes of the canons, who had holed up in their cloister, and he threatened to kill them in order to make them bow to his will. Geoffrey of Lèves had fled and feared for his life—for good reason. Robert was called in by the canons as a last resort, "the only hope other than God." Despite the illness that had laid him low again, the master went forth. "Everything is possible for me unto death," he told those asking him to come. He spoke to the two parties and calmed them down. Thibaud agreed to recognize the election of Geoffrey of Lèves, who returned. At the reconciler's insistence, the canons (we must imagine some of them were susceptible to the count's pressure) made a solemn oath never again to tolerate simony, "this execrable plague . . . that had for a very long time defiled their Church." Twenty years later, Robert remained faithful to the mission Pope Urban II had entrusted to him.

Robert had no fear of Thibaud's power. Leaving Chartres in the company of Bernard of Tiron, he set out for Blois, the count's capital, to visit William of Nevers. This faithful vassal of the king had been imprisoned while defending royal rights. For the time being, he languished in the victor's dungeon. William of Nevers was a saintly warrior. He died in 1148 as a monk of La Chartreuse. Bernard and Robert held the "religious count" in high regard. On seeing the two, William exclaimed, "Who would not rejoice to be long imprisoned in order that he could be visited by such men?"

So now they toured together the world that both wanted to flee so much. For a long time, the same desire had driven them. More than once—in the desert of Craon, on the preachers' paths, at the Council of Poitiers in 1100—they had found themselves side by side. From Blois, the one set off toward the south while the other returned to Tiron. They did not know that this parting in January 1116 was the last time they would see each other in this life.

Robert and his little troop journeyed toward Orsan, a priory of Fontevraud in Berry, when suddenly thieves set on them. It was the horses they wanted, failing other riches. The brothers all ended up on the ground. Robert, thrown down from his mount and beaten by the thieves, exhorted them "with the voice of a dove" to renounce their life of crime, worrying "more about their perdition than the insults heaped on him." For Peter, one of Robert's companions, this was too much. "Don't you know that this man you've just knocked off his horse is Robert of Arbrissel, whose sweet fragrance of holiness spreads over the whole world?" At Robert's name, the band of thieves, in sudden terror, threw themselves at the feet of the great man, begging his forgiveness. Smiling and splendid in his mildness, Robert granted it and kissed them.

These little episodes, tales within the tale that the hagiographer serves up as a delightful dessert, usually have some literary echo. They are exemplary in that they are edifying, but also because they are examples from a long series. Not that it was impossible to have unfortunate encounters on medieval highways—far from it; but the thief who falls without warning under the influence of learned men automatically recalls the thieves who set on St. Martin of Tours in the Alps. "Are you afraid?" asked the one who was charged with robbing him. Martin replied that he had never felt so safe, relying as he did on the mercy of the Lord, but that he felt sorry for the robber for being so cut off from that mercy.[16] Behind the story of Martin is the silhouette of Scripture, which tells us to love our enemies. So Peter's holy anger is more than just that, for it gives the episode its own life. Peter duly reported to Andreas both the episode and its literary nature, complete with biblical citations. It is a good bet that he didn't leave out a word.

Finally the troop arrived in safe harbor at the priory of Orsan. Robert spent two weeks there, waiting for Petronilla, from whom he had been parted at Hautes-Bruyères. When she arrived he departed along with her, because once more he had been asked to come preach at a place Andreas does not specify, but to the north, perhaps toward Orléans.[17] On the way he stopped at Déols, an old

16. Sulpicius Severus, "Life of Martin of Tours," in *Early Christian Lives,* trans. White, 140 (section 5).

17. Robert's last, abbreviated preaching tour, discussed in detail in the pages that follow, is recounted in Andreas, *Second Life,* sections 22–26 (PL 162: 1068–1070; Venarde, *Robert of Arbrissel,* 37–40).

Benedictine monastery adjacent to the town of Châteauroux. The monks welcomed him joyfully, and the next day, at their insistence, he called them together and inspired them with the Word. He took advantage of this sojourn to settle a property dispute between Fontevraud and Déols and at the same time reconcile the monks to Lord Alard, the protector of Fontevraud's priory of Orsan. When Petronilla and Angarde departed for the motherhouse, continuing this strange ballet in which Robert heart's desire seemed to be to leave the nuns as soon as he found them, he slipped away with his chaplain Andreas to the people who awaited his preaching.

Saints are made such by others. God's chosen have no power, from one point of view, except with the consent of people. There is no sanctity without some sort of process, formal or informal. A *vita* written in honor of the candidate for sanctity was a major part of the process, still in Robert's day not yet wholly controlled and regulated by the papacy. Andreas knew this well. In the meanderings of this final tour and the anecdotes just repeated, the hagiographer did not stray for a second. These detours would be insignificant if they did not constitute, just below the surface, a learned discourse on virtues.

The *vita* is also a plea that preemptively warded off attacks. To counter the image of Robert as troublemaker and scandal-bearer, Andreas carefully juxtaposes a sage of undisputed eminence, a "peacemaker" and "mediator of disputes." In less than four months, Robert pacified four disputes, including the serious troubles at Chartres. "For the Lord had conferred such grace on him that not only did religious people venerate him but even kings and princes willingly followed his orders."[18] There is no recognized sanctity without rumor of sanctity. A cult did no more than officially ratify a renown that emerged from the accretion of evidence. What better

18. Andreas, *Second Life*, section 16 (PL 162: 1065; Venarde, *Robert of Arbrissel*, 34).

argument, from that perspective, than recognition by the robbers and the tremble of shame that overtook them at the mention of Robert's name? Nor should we believe that only friendship was involved in the visit to William of Nevers. The collection would hardly have been complete if Robert had not visited prisoners (to be surer to be glorified on Judgment Day),[19] nor did the brigands appear as noted except to prove his capacity to forgive his enemies.

Whenever we would like to understand the man, we are presented with the saint. On the other hand, the power that his sermons radiated, the very personal talent for correcting and affecting that was clamored for from one end of France to the other and that, according to Andreas, left hearers gasping and gaping because it managed to speak at the same time to all and to each individual—is that not a singular trait that distinguishes him from all the archetypes? "His preaching, far from being ineffective, so struck the hearts of his audience that it was quite clear who was there. The Holy Spirit was wholly present, without whose aid the speech of a learned man labors in vain, concerning which it is written, 'It is not you who speak, but the spirit of your Father.'"[20] The citation from Matthew's Gospel sums up the whole hagiographic enterprise. Far from unveiling competing idols or even retracing individual destinies, each *vita* attributes to a common source the individual's merits that are exemplary because of the example of Christ. Therefore, the week that now began, from February 18 to February 25, was an imitation of Holy Week, just as Robert's last stops were stations on the road to the cross.

---

19. See Mt 25:36, 39, 44, part of a sermon about Judgment Day when charitable acts including visiting prisoners will help to separate sheep from goats.

20. Andreas, *Second Life*, section 23 (PL 162: 1069; Venarde, *Robert of Arbrissel*, 38). The quotation is from Mt 10:20.

A GATHERING AT ORSAN

The Friday he left Déols, Robert's illness worsened and obliged him to dismount from his horse repeatedly.[21] His companions, the first to sense what was going to happen, urged him to return to Orsan. However, Robert persisted and wanted to push on to the nearby citadel of Graçay as a token of goodwill for the people who awaited him. The party arrived and the lord of the place offered them hospitality. By the morning, the illness had worsened and Robert could no longer ride. This time, he decided to turn back. "Dear brothers, make a wooden litter for me and carry me back to Orsan, for I know I am going to die from this illness." His host quickly said, "Please, master, do not do as you say, but instead stay here until you see if you can be relieved of your pain." Robert immediately told his brothers, privately, "Whatever anyone says, pay no mind, but do what I told you!" They got as far as the castle of Issoudun with the makeshift litter. The castellan offered hospitality and tried the same ploy; the host hovered around the moribund master, trying to get him to stay. "Take me back to Orsan," ordered Robert as soon as he heard about this scheme.

Finally, on Sunday, the band of brothers reached the priory directed by Agnes, the estranged wife of the local lord, Alard of Châteaumeillant. Haste had truly worn them out; they covered the twenty miles from Graçay to Issoudun in one day and some twenty-seven the next day, from Issoudun to Orsan, toting an improvised stretcher on which the dying Robert rolled at every bump. Scarcely arrived, he regretted his actions. The day of Sunday, February 20, drew to a close. Robert lamented softly. "Oh Fontevraud, Fontevraud, how I dreamed of lying in you!" The faithful Andreas

21. Andreas, *Second Life*, sections 24–26 (PL 162: 1069–1070; Venarde, *Robert of Arbrissel*, 39–40), describe Friday, February 18; Saturday, February 19; and Sunday, February 20, 1116.

approached. "Great master, what are you saying? If you think that the end has come, at least do your soul's desire and order that your body should be carried to Fontevraud after your death." Robert replied, "What good would it do to carry my corpse away from here? It would be taken away from you at some little place." Andreas stresses that these were Robert's exact words.

At the first signs of the final agony, Robert had clearly become prey. His manifest holiness made his body into a potential relic. People of the age had enormous passion for relics. To see them, even better to touch them, was to ensure the saint's protection and above all the healing for which the faithful prayed. It did not matter if the relics were small scraps, since their magical power, the beneficial force that flowed from them, was no less intense for that. Prestigious fragments from the Holy Land commanded the price of gold. In the thirteenth century, St. Louis, the king of France, would pay more than three times more for the Crown of Thorns than to build the Sainte-Chapelle to house it.[22] The credulity of some laid them open to fraud. Specialized workshops soon grew up to manufacture these invaluable talismans. One of the surest means of having authentic relics was theft or, better still, seizure of the remains while they were still warm. What better guarantee of authenticity and therefore effectiveness? In 397, St. Martin died at Candes. The citizens of Poitou wanted to profit from this windfall by seizing his body, but a group from Tours, eluding Poitevin vigilance, hauled it out the window of the church where it lay guarded.[23] When the inhabitants of Saint-Michel-de-Cuxa saw Romuald take to bed, they

22. The Sainte-Chapelle, on the Ile de la Cité in Paris, remains a spectacular example of Gothic architecture.

23. Gregory of Tours, *History of the Franks*, trans. Lewis Thorpe (Harmondsworth, 1974), 97–99 (Book I, section 48). Gregory, a late sixth-century bishop of Tours, was a devotee of his predecessor and wrote extensively about St. Martin's miracles as well as making him a focal point of the early part of his chronicle of the Frankish peoples.

wanted to finish him off so as not to lose his remains.[24] Carrying the body of their founder Vitalis back to Savigny, the monks had to resist the greed of the inhabitants of the small village of Teilleul, who wanted to keep it.[25] As for William Firmatus, his death set off a battle between the armies of Domfort, Mayenne, and Mortain.[26]

As soon as Robert's death approached, the lords of Berry, men of an age when every warrior was something of a looter, began to circle over the holy men like vultures. The brothers immediately feared that the holy body would slip out of their control. The master himself had compromised everything by wishing to push on to the north to preach before yielding a day later. The delay is telling; in this still muddled mixture of primitive religiosity and the preaching of the good news, Robert alone placed the message he delivered above the magical power of his body.

Robert now had to think about another journey. On Monday, he asked for "the viaticum of the body and blood of Our Lord Jesus Christ," those travel provisions "without which the traveler, condemned to wander, always goes astray."[27] Before receiving the Eucharist, he made a long public confession "with inner groans and deep sighs." The next day he asked for extreme unction and, again, communion, not without once again reproaching himself "more than any bandit ever did." As it is written, Andreas recalls, "The righteous man is his own first accuser."[28]

This same Tuesday, the little priory of Orsan entertained a mob it could scarcely contain. At Orsan, the medieval buildings are

24. *Petri Damiani vita beati Romualdi*, ed. Tabacco, 35 (section 13); trans. Leyser in Head, ed., *Medieval Hagiography*, 301.

25. Etienne de Fougères, *Vita B. Vitalis*, 384.

26. Etienne de Fougères (?), *Vita S. Firmati*, section 27 (Pigeon, *Vies des saints*, 2: 394–395 [French translation], 414 [Latin text]; AASS April, volume 3, 335).

27. The events of Monday, February 21, and Tuesday, February 22, are recounted in Andreas, *Second Life*, sections 27–30 (PL 162: 1070–1072; Venarde, *Robert of Arbrissel*, 40–43).

28. Prv 18:17.

gone, replaced by elegant sixteenth-century constructions. In the meadow, along a stream, still visible at the beginning of the twentieth century were the bases of pillars where the sisters' chapel had once been; a few steps away, thicker and greener grass signaled the site of the ponds that supplied this little world with fish. For the rest—the sisters' home—there would have been a large farmhouse that never sheltered more than a dozen people. At a distance, and even more basic, were the brothers' huts. Founded in 1107, this priory was at the start hastily erected out of wood for arrivals from Fontevraud. During the time Agnes was prioress, more permanent construction began. Whenever it was finished, it was still a very modest shelter for the high society that crowded around on this Tuesday, February 22, 1116.[29]

First among them was Leger, the archbishop of Bourges. A dozen years earlier he had struck up a friendship with the founder of Fontevraud. Interested in welcoming a priory of the federation into his diocese, he surveyed the region for a suitable place. Since the foundation of Orsan, Leger had kept a paternal eye on the nuns. Robert had asked the archbishop to come to his bedside. News of the holy man's mortal agony had spread and the lords of the country followed on the archbishop's heels. The first precaution, as much the archbishop's as the warriors', was to surround the priory with armed men to make sure that this gift of heaven would not escape them. After that, there was still time to take in piously the teachings of the dying man.

Then came Petronilla and Angarde. Robert had asked for them to be summoned on Saturday. The messenger, sent from Graçay to ride flat out, caught up with them at La Puye, another house of Fontevraud where they were lodging on the way home. He arrived

29. F. Deshoulières, "Le prieuré d'Orsan en Berri," *Mémoires de la société des antiquaires du Centre* 25 (1901), 88–98, contains descriptions of the compound as of a century ago, with a sketch map between pages 88 and 89 (reproduced in Dalarun, *L'impossible saintété*, 170).

in the middle of Sunday night, having covered about seventy-five miles in barely twenty-four hours. He told the two women to make haste. They did not wait for daylight and on Tuesday evening they finished the journey of ninety miles that had separated them from Orsan. They must have been exhausted. "Alas, good master, you will do us no more good!" exclaimed Petronilla. Angarde corrected her. "Do not say that, good woman, but instead pray God that He deem it worthy to preserve his health. He who has given Robert this illness will grant him health when it pleases Him." Was Petronilla tending to bury the master a little too quickly? In any case, Andreas forgave her nothing and took pleasure in telling how her second in command lectured her.

LAST WISHES

This was no time for internal dissension. Given the latent war in which each side had just taken its position, the Fontevraud party needed all its forces. On Wednesday, Robert tried his luck.[30] He summoned Leger and began a long speech. He first reminded the archbishop of the love that united them, Leger's insistence on having nuns of Fontevraud come to his diocese, and the care he had always taken for them. These were only preliminaries.

"Furthermore, I want to tell your friendship of my heart's desire, I want to reveal it to your holiness. Let it show forth at my death if you loved me when I was alive and if I was ever dear to you as you said. You are not unaware that true affection is not only in words but, as Holy Scripture testifies, the proof of love is in works. 'Let us not love in word or speech, but in deed and truth.'[31] So I make it known to you, dearest father, that I do not want to lie in Bethlehem, where God deigned to be

---

30. This day's events are the focus of Andreas, *Second Life*, chapters 31–45 (PL 162: 1072–1078 and Dalarun, *L'impossible sainteté*, 284–286; Venarde, *Robert of Arbrissel*, 43–52).

31. 1 Jn 3:18.

born of the Virgin, nor at the Holy Sepulcher in Jerusalem. No more do I want to be buried in Rome among the holy martyrs or at the monastery of Cluny where gorgeous processions take place. . . . I do not want to be buried anywhere except Fontevraud. You know, my father, that I made Fontevraud the head of all the other places. The greatest part of our congregation is there, the core of our religion is there. I do not ask you to bury me in the monastery or the cloister, but just among my little brothers in the mud of Fontevraud. There are my priests and clergy; there too are the holy virgins, widows, and chaste women, persevering day and night in the praise of God. There are my dear sick ones, men and women, there are my lepers, male and female. There are the good companions of my wandering, those who for Christ's sake bore poverty and travail along with me. There are those who patiently suffered cold and heat, miseries and tribulations, for the salvation of their souls, who at the call of my preaching, inspired by God, gave themselves up and left their property. Some of them are still alive and others are dead, having persevered in obedience to the end. There lies the nun Hersende, my good assistant, with whose advice and labor I raised the buildings at Fontevraud. There lie my good sons to whose prayers I entrust intercession before God. There sleep my good nuns, by whose merits I believe I am helped before God. Here is why, dear friend, I decline entombment in holier places: I greatly desire to be buried in the mud beside my little brothers and sisters. I know that when they were alive, they wanted me to lie in this place so that on the day of Resurrection, I would go peacefully with them in this same flesh to the judgment of God."

What energy Robert showed in reaching Orsan! Lost in a foreign territory, watched on all sides by predators, he made it his priority to find refuge in a house of his order. From Graçay, Orsan was the closest dependent house of Fontevraud and therefore the destination of Robert and his companions. By calculation and by reflex they retraced their steps. In safe harbor, the master gave himself to dreaming of the motherhouse, without first daring to believe it. He could also count up errors made in haste: Graçay was eight miles from the Cher River and it would have sufficed to give himself up to the watercourse to get back to Fontevraud. However, now Petronilla had come and he knew that he could rely on her determination. If the barons of Berry had posted their guard, the monks and nuns surely went to impress a crowd of new recruits from neighboring monasteries. Finally, Robert hoped he had touched Leger's heart, in the name of their long friendship, with his speech.

Why did the desire for Fontevraud grip him so strongly? First of all, he saw an internal necessity for his congregation; unity could be sealed forever over his body. Robert's Fontevraud was extremely centralized. He had wanted it so when he named an abbess for it but forbade anything but prioresses in the other communities. The remains of the founder, brought back to the central place, would remind every house that it was but a member of the body of which Fontevraud was the head.

There were other dissensions to fear even more in this religious city that the dying man described with emotion and pride. A monastic town is what the great Loire abbey still appears to be today, even if of the five original structures only three survive—the Great Monastery, Saint Benedict, and Saint Lazarus—while the Magdalene and Saint John have been destroyed. A city is all white or all black, either Jerusalem or Babylon. Fontevraud would be Babel if division arose, if the brothers balked again, if each category of seekers flew apart in centrifugal motion. It would be a heavenly city, however, if harmony reigned among parties who called for unity because they arranged diversity in complementary couples: the sick and the hale, men and women, virgins and converts. In the mixed order of Sempringham, the holy body of the founder, Gilbert, was embedded in the wall that divided the nave of the abbey church into two parts, one for men and one for women. Lying between them, he was the link.[32] That was Robert's dream: who in my

32. The Order of St. Gilbert of Sempringham, centered in the English county of Lincolnshire and with many similarities to the Order of Fontevraud, took shape

congregation, he thought, has a heart so hard that when thinking of me, he would not let himself dissolve in sighs and tears? Better than statutes, better than constraint, the holy body sealed at Fontevraud would remind all of their peculiar arrangement, for around it the lushness of creation would order itself in a perfect cosmogony. Is it not over relics that one swore oaths? Nothing could better guarantee faith.

There was also something more intimate, a more secret motivation that resulted in Robert's final wish. The structure of a biography lies in the passage of dates that give emphasis. The composition of a hagiographic account, as Michel de Certeau puts it, is much more a composition of *places*.[33] If a biography, moving through time, is necessarily a one-way trip, a saint's Life is an intentionally cyclical journey and thereby harbors in its very nature the promise of eternity. The *Life of Alexis* follows this pattern, since the entire odyssey of the hero is a return to the point of departure for an ultimate epiphany. Robert, in an earlier time, dreamed of fulfilling this trajectory of the prodigal son to his native land.[34] Everything that drew him away from Arbrissel only prepared for a more brilliant day of triumphal return. In leaving La Roë, where he had gotten so close to the goal, he muddied the meaning of his own story. It was no longer of recovering his inheritance that he dreamed, but of conquering unknown lands.

During the entire early Middle Ages, sainthood was only the fulfillment of God's initial choice. "Saints are born, not made," said Honorius Augustodunensis as late as the twelfth century, showing that the old idea lasted a very long time.[35] Among Robert's genera-

---

in the 1130s, 1140s, and 1150s. See Brian Golding, *Gilbert of Sempringham and the Gilbertine Order, c. 1130–c. 1300* (Oxford, 1995).

33. Michel de Certeau, *The Writing of History*, trans. Tom Conley (New York, 1988), 281.

34. For the parable of the prodigal son, see Lk 15:11–32.

35. Quoted in André Vauchez, *The Spirituality of the Medieval West: From the*

tion, a new sensibility emerged, a sanctity of becoming, of conquest "by the sweat of one's brow," as André Vauchez aptly puts it. Robert's life was exceptional because it contains this transition, describing in turn, with the lure of places, the trajectory of nostalgia *and* the call of a new world. Robert could not bear to suffer exclusion from this virgin territory once he had found it, tamed it, and mapped it out. Who is not outraged to see Moses die at the threshold of the Promised Land, forbidden to go in?[36]

None of these calculations would have made any sense if Robert had not carried within himself, along with the ideas of both his own guilt and his own worth, the certainty that he would be acknowledged a saint. Andreas's account for some pages rests on the premise, audible even as a whisper, that this body, now wearing out and therefore taking up ever more space, belonged to one of God's chosen. The twelfth century constituted a hiatus in this regard. Before then, as André Vauchez emphasizes, there was not yet a regular canonization procedure and therefore sanctity was awarded readily; a few hardships endured, thieves who prostrated themselves, an exemplary death and—voila!—the title is granted.[37] Then came the idea that consecration was earned and won rather than fallen from heaven. Escaping from both predestination and from falling wholly under the power of the Church, there was a generation that could, with some chance of success, settle on the project of becoming a saint. This project, in hagiographic discourse, was expressed as a trajectory, a parabola.

Fontevraud was now Robert's territory of choice. Michel de Certeau says that hagiography, the "geography of the sacred" that revolves around a foundational place of birth or death, functions to

Eighth to the Twelfth Century, trans. Colette Friedlander (Kalamazoo, MI, 1993), 150.

36. See Dt 32:51–52 and 34:1–5.

37. André Vauchez, *Sainthood in the Later Middle Ages*, trans. Jean Birrell (New York, 1997), 13–21.

designate a "non-place," a "spiritual space," and a "beyond." Minute attention to location speaks, at base, to something that cannot be located.[38] More prosaically, hagiographic literature fulfills another function: to make ordinary places of the West into sacred ones. So in Robert's paean, the litany of rejected places—Bethlehem, Jerusalem, and Rome—has as its counterpoint the humble tune of Fontevraud, its mud, brothers, and sisters. Like an incantation, the name of Fontevraud, which he prefers even to Cluny with its grand processions, comes seven times to the lips of the dying man. There could be no clearer or franker statement of the gap between the two ideals embodied in these abbeys as heads of monastic orders. There is no shadow of contempt or critique, only the distance that separates two planets. Key, too, is the repetition of the terms "lie," "be buried," and "in the mud" as indication of Robert's desire to merge with the soil, like a seed. The great Gospel figures were the first, according to legend, to come to cultivate pagan territories: Peter in Rome, James at Compostella, Mary Magdalene at Vézelay, Denis in the Ile-de-France. Little by little, native saints completed the work, and between two ends of the process lay the space of daily life. Where Robert would be buried holiness would take root and sprout; hence the extreme importance of everyone agreeing to his burial at Fontevraud.

Archbishop Leger was the first to shy away.

"You know, dear father, that I have loved you with my whole being for a very long time. What you ask me is not wholly in my power but to a great extent depends on the princes of this region. You know that this place is in the territory of a certain lord named Alard, who in large part built it. I do not want to make any promises I cannot keep afterwards. But tomorrow, discuss the matter without me."

Andreas, who knew his master's desire, quickly stepped in. Agnes, the prioress of Orsan, was a native of the region and Alard was her

38. Certeau, *Writing of History*, 282.

husband; she could greatly help or greatly hinder the undertaking. Robert summoned her and was solemn.

"Oh, Lady Agnes!" Nun as she was, she remained the wife of a lord, a *domina* whose office of prioress only kept the social order in place. "Oh, Lady Agnes, I prayerfully command and commandingly pray you as my lady, my daughter, and my disciple, to do whatever is in your power concerning the matter I have asked the archbishop to do."

"Good master, you want me to do this?"

"I want this absolutely, my daughter, and I desire it and I bid you to kiss my hand to seal the pact."

Torn between two interests, obedience to her master and loyalty to her native province, Agnes promised with the press of her lips.

LAST AGONIES

At this point, death tightened its grip. Those around Robert prompted him to pray. "I very much desire to pray to God but I cannot do so at all because you are in the way. Withdraw and depart so I can pray to my God in peace!" For the time being, Robert preferred contemplation to the death that everyone openly awaited, desiring a deep and intimate submersion instead of a grand spectacle. Nevertheless, a small group of intimates stayed around him. He required not solitude but intimacy. He bent himself to prayer for the pope, the teachers of the Church, his hosts, his benefactors, and then his enemies, ending with William of Aquitaine, that he might return to "the way of truth." William's is the only name mentioned, as if the duke were Robert's mirror image and his alter ego.

The prayers continued. In the silence of the night, he called Peter, not the priest who was with him when the thieves had assaulted him, but a lay brother who served him. "Call the priest Andreas to me!" When Andreas arrived, Robert said, "Bring me, I pray you, the wood of the holy cross!" With great difficulty he rose and, facing the cross, knelt to say his Credo in the sight of those with him, mentioning creation, incarnation, and redemption before concluding by thanking God for the mercies He had conferred. Still at the foot of the cross, he now accused himself. "Priest, hear my sins; hear them, heaven and earth! The Son of God came into this world to save sinners, of whom I am the foremost. I was conceived in wickedness and nurtured in sins and I have sinned in countless ways through my own fault." The five sins he named took him rapidly through the stages of his life. When he was a boy and his mother fed him, he wanted the better portions. When it rained, he wanted it dry, and vice versa—such was the desire of the peasant he must have been while acting as parish priest of Arbrissel. Robert accused himself of simony in the election of a bishop of Rennes. He had not made full use of "the great knowledge of literature and grace in preaching" that God had given. He had allowed himself to be praised for his foundation, although the merit in it came from the women that he had gathered. Absolved by the priest, he asked God to deliver him from this world and commended his company to His care. The cross was removed and all went to sleep.[39]

The death Robert awaited did not come, but in the darkness the forces of evil grew bolder. "Woe to you, impious crowd! Why are you here? Get back, as God commands!" While the others slept on, only Robert struggled. Peter woke up and thought his master was delirious. Robert denied it, annoyed that anyone doubt the reality of the assault. Agnes, terrified, had heard everything in the confined space where Robert lay. A throng of enemies had come to attack him. She quickly crossed herself. Were they still there? No, he had dispatched them with the sign of the cross. What were they

39. It is at this point that the Latin text breaks off; the rest of this chapter relies on the late medieval French version of Andreas's *vita*. See above, chapter 1, and below, chapter 6. Instead of translating from the Latin versions, Dalarun reproduced the French of ca. 1500 when quoting, starting in the next paragraph.

like, she wondered. "They were blacker than coal and dressed like monks." Distrustful, she asked the basic question. "How did they dare to come to you? Did they think they would find something of which to accuse you?" He replied, "Surely they thought that I should die like a beast and for that reason they came here, in vain, to lie in wait and take advantage of me. For like it or not, with God's help I shall die like a good Christian."

The process is by now familiar. As if on a palimpsest, this account hides another. "What are you doing here, bloody brute? You will find nothing in me, cursed one! Abraham's breast receives me."[40] Once again, the dossier on St. Martin provides the key to this little episode set in Andreas's narration. The connections between the two saints would intensify. Martin, of course, was the nearly obligatory prototype for a figure like Robert. The first apostle to the Gauls in the fourth century, he took up the challenge of the Egyptian fathers, proving that the banks of the Loire had no need to envy the solitude of the desert.[41] Martin founded the two oldest monasteries in Gaul, Ligugé and Marmoutier. Every other hermit, every other monastic founder was a bit of an imitator. His prestige was such that his friend Sulpicius Severus took the very unusual step of writing his *vita* before Martin died. Afterwards, Sulpicius sensed the need to complete his unfinished account and did so in a letter addressed to his stepmother Bassula.[42] This detailed letter, meant from the beginning for the widest possible distribution, was thereafter the implicit reference for holy deaths. Andreas was all the more drawn to it because, in completing the work of Baudri, he was, just like the letter to Bassula, describing a death more than a life. In spite of this, starting with Agnes's final ques-

40. PL 20: 183, from a letter by Martin's biographer Sulpicius Severus to his stepmother Bassula.

41. Sulpicius Severus, "Life of Martin of Tours," in *Early Christian Lives*, trans. White, 144 (section 10).

42. Complete text in PL 20: 180–184.

tion, the chaplain glosses at length the meaning of the episode Robert had just made current again.

The Enemy pursued saints to avenge the insults to which he was ceaselessly subjected by holy people. He knew well that after their death, the just would escape him and, seeing them at the brink of death, he tried to take advantage of their weakness to harass them. The last moments were therefore the most dangerous and Martin died repelling the final assault. Leaving aside for a moment these legendary battles, Andreas legitimately asks, "If the Enemy had wanted to obliterate and obstruct one of the principle lights of the Church, do we think in the least that he will not strive to obstruct and terrify us as much as he possibly can? For this reason, our only hope rests in the hand of Our Lord, through which He in His mercy will be able to deliver us from the Enemy's power."

Paradoxically, the ordinary mortal has less to fear than the saint. The former has divine power to shelter his weakness, but the latter is left on his own, abandoned by God. At Yahweh's court, Satan came forward. "Where have you been?"

"Prowling around the earth."

"Did you notice my servant Job? There is nobody like him on earth: an honest and righteous man who fears God and guards against evil."

Satan replied, "Lay a finger on him and, I swear, he will curse you to your face."

"So be it," said Yahweh to Satan, "he is in your power. Just let him live."[43] God's champion is thrown back on his own resources. The one whose colors he defends consents to his testing. The saint is far from being in the lead in this clash of titans. A sick man, not an athlete, crawls along. Therefore if he carries off great victories, it is not because of a magnificent performance, but because everything is infinitely worse for him. To rejoin the common lot of hu-

43. Jb 1:6–12.

mankind becomes a feat and his ambition pathetic: "I will die like a good Christian" and not "like a beast." Belatedly assisted by Christ against a pack of demons, St. Anthony groaned, "Where were you, good Jesus, where were you? Why didn't you stand with me from the start to tend my wounds?" A voice answered, "I was there, Anthony, but I was waiting to see you fight. From now on, because you did not cease to resist manfully, I will help you always and make your name known everywhere."[44]

This abandonment at which the saint despairs in fact carries along with it the promise of fame for him and redemption for others. Robert, who watched while all around him slept, relived the beginning of Christ's Passion in Gethsemane. His disciples have left Him alone in the dark and even He weakens for a moment. "Father, if you want, take this cup away from me." On the cross, like a cry of pain, He sang, "My God, my God, why have you forsaken me?"—a psalm that arose in the course of the night but ended up as a triumphal anthem.[45]

Robert brought his own contribution to this collection of stories. No Satan, no devil or demon, but the Enemy, dressed "in monastic habit"—his own. Not content to be his own first accuser, he always saw in himself his worst enemy.

Daybreak dispersed dreams and business resumed.[46] Agnes had kept her promise and Alard presented himself to the dying man on this Thursday. Robert took up his plea at once: the tie of friendship, his arrival in Berry without any resources, the initial offering by the lord of Orsan. "Under the authority of your good

44. Athanasius, "The Life of Anthony," in *Early Christian Lives*, trans. White, 16 (section 10).

45. Mt 26:36–46 recounts Jesus' moment of weakness; Mt 27:46 and Mk 15:34 report Jesus' quotation of Psalm 21/22:1, which starts in despair before turning to praise of Yahweh.

46. Andreas, *Second Life*, sections 46–50 (Dalarun, *L'impossible sainteté*, 286–289; Venarde, *Robert of Arbrissel*, 52–56), recounts the events of Thursday, February 24.

archbishop Leger, for the salvation of your soul and those of your relations, you gave me this deserted place to build a little lodging for the handmaids of Jesus Christ." Copied in its essentials from the address to Leger, this speech nonetheless differed in tactic. With the archbishop, Robert had very cleverly contrasted return to Fontevraud not with burial in Berry but with one in holy sites. Evading the real question, he appeared to take counsel with his friend concerning a decision that concerned only him and his order. With Alard, there was no more evasion. Time was pressing and Robert's tone grew sharper. "I know that the inhabitants of this land will want me to be buried here. But for myself, I do not want to be anywhere other than the cemetery at Fontevraud." Agnes's husband made his declarations of friendship, but replied that only "my lords of Bourges, Raoul of Déols, and Geoffrey of Issoudun" had power over the matter.

Orsan was effectively a co-foundation. Alard, the direct lord of the place, gave his land to Robert, but also placed it under the power of Leger as co-sponsor of the enterprise. To do this, Alard had to get the permission of his own lord, Raoul the Elder of Déols, who dominated a large section of western Berry while the archbishop controlled, none too effectively, the eastern section of the province. The priory of Orsan was on the border of these two areas. In a charter of 1113, the chief lords of Berry pledged to respect the nuns' properties; at the head of the list were Raoul of Déols and Geoffrey of Issoudun, his most loyal vassal, but there were also the lords of Saint-Sévère, Huriel, and Lignières. Such a pact was hardly overkill. In the first year of his reign, 1108, King Louis VI had to come punish the formidable Humbaud of Saint-Sévère, who kept the country under his thumb; with his own hand, Louis had dispatched the rebel in the ditch of his own castle.[47]

47. On the balance of power in Berry, see Dalarun, *L'impossible sainteté*, 159–171 passim. For a twelfth-century account of the humiliation of Humbaud, see

As Robert lay dying, Geoffrey of Issoudun was at Orsan. Geoffrey had been the overly attentive host who, the previous Saturday, wanted to confiscate the saint's remains; apparently he followed the tracks as if hunting down prey. Raoul was not there and Robert understood that Alard was playing the same game as the archbishop: using jurisdictional confusion as an excuse, sending the matter back from one side to the other until death ensued. Robert lost his nerve and ordered Petronilla to have a litter prepared for him so he could be carried back to Fontevraud still alive. Alard was threatening that the people would not let it happen. In a final curse, Robert begged his adversary to give up his advantage. He was through with arguments. The dying man's fit of anger must have been fairly dreadful for Alard to give way. Alard promised to take the body as far as the lands of the count of Anjou and sealed this agreement hand-in-hand with Robert. Snarling, the lord of Orsan warned Petronilla that she should be on guard with the neighboring count "and that it would cause great misfortune, after Robert died in their land, that others not of their land should have the consolation for it." Robert remained wary and told the abbess to appeal to Rome if anyone tried to block the transfer of his body.

Then the whole convent invaded the little room where Robert lay at rest. "Alas, our good father, very soon you will leave us desolate orphans." The young women gathered around him in tears; he caressed them with his hand. What he said, though, was singularly at odds with this tender gesture; as much as he hoped for deliverance, he would still support them if he could. Andreas does not hesitate to wax rhapsodic about this little speech as if it were a show of the greatest sacrifice. Robert went on at length. He "would have lived excellently in religion if divine pity had not constrained him to come to the aid of their weakness." For him, happiness was else-

Suger, *The Deeds of Louis the Fat*, trans. Richard Cusimano and John Moorhead (Washington, DC, 1992), 59–60.

where, "to live an utterly solitary life and live in the desert in hunger, thirst, and nakedness . . . always to wear a hairshirt and go barefoot to preach the Word of God and content himself only that listeners be given to him and that they might welcome what his nature had finally demanded." For the gratified founder, the desert and wandering would always be, like Mary's, the better part—and his foundation a burden.

Robert would die the next day, Friday, February 25, 1116, since his Savior died on that day of the week. Everyone knew it and events moved more quickly.[48] The brothers pressed in as a group, in a planned approach, and begged him to tell them their duty. Robert got annoyed. "Surely, my brothers, if for a long time I had not taught you how you should live and what you should do, it would be far too late now!" Still, one last time, he rapped out orders. "Obey the handmaids of Jesus Christ through your entire lives, for the salvation of your souls, and serve them for the love of their bridegroom Jesus Christ." This last request is strange. Apparently the brothers hoped to get some kind of softening of their fate; but those who had rejected female supremacy had left in the autumn. What did the rest want? Robert's response was two-fold: obey to ensure salvation and serve for love, not of the women but of their Lord. Here was the best courtly tradition in which, as Georges Duby has pointed out, love was an affair between men.[49] The brothers, in a wholly chivalric spirit, very much desired the humility of freely granted service. They refused the humiliation of subjected obedience. Through his entire narrative, Andreas faithfully reports the remarks of the master, but when he let himself go to talk about his own lord, when he poured forth his heart, he al-

48. Events on Friday, February 25, are recounted in Andreas, *Second Life*, sections 51–55 (Dalarun, *L'impossible saintété*, 289–291; Venarde, *Robert of Arbrissel*, 56–58).

49. Georges Duby, *William Marshall: The Flower of Chivalry*, trans. Richard Howard (New York, 1985), 47.

ways exalted the service of John the Evangelist and failed to mention obedience. In doing that, he must have been communicating the sentiment of his brothers.

Right on their heels, worried about this men's meeting, the women's hierarchy came forward and asked Robert the same question, with the same feigned naiveté. "How should we live after your death?" The decision came down: "Do nothing new without the counsel of your religious brothers." Certainly they would have been frustrated. So what did they want? Power? Other women's houses offered that, but they had chosen Fontevraud, its difficulties, and its uncertainties. So why did they balk at this right of control granted to men? They had accepted from Robert a service that flattered them. The simultaneous expansion in their social milieu of "fine amor," the cult of love service by men to women, shows that such a sensibility was latent in court and cloister, ready to burst forth. However, after the death of the master who fascinated them and held them in a thrall that never failed, these ladies could only be the instrument of salvation for the brothers, in their eyes men without prestige, socially contemptible.

As for Robert, he remained on the same tightrope as always. Serve and obey at the same time, he said to the men, because he thought the humiliation of obedience better for salvation than the humility of service. Do not change the rules without counsel, he said to the women, because his ascetic project for men demanded that the door to freedom remain ajar, that humiliation be desired before being imposed. It was an impossible wager that no statute, no oath, not even the talisman of the founder's relics could guarantee. Until the French Revolution suppressed it, the Order of Fontevraud echoed with the noise of quarrelling. The exception that was Robert himself could not become a general rule.

The last to come forward was Andreas, our narrator. As soon as he saw him, Robert said, "Surely I can talk no longer and my senses fail. So hasten to ask me what you want." Was this because

the dying man was fainting? In any case, the dialogue was brief.
Robert began another prayer, a Miserere, and then fell silent. Andreas picked up a candle, since the room was dim, a holy taper that
perhaps gave the dying man a measure of the time he had left.[50]
The chaplain held the flame close to his master's face and saw he
had lost consciousness. In tears, he hastily assembled the brothers
and sisters. Robert came to, said a Confiteor for them, and absolved
them with a Pater Noster for penance.[51] He commended his soul to
God. "And thus, making the sign of the cross for himself and for his
flock, amidst the tears of his brothers and the lamentations of his
sons, he died and gave over his devout soul to Our Lord on that
Friday at the hour of Vespers."

THE DIVISION OF THE SPOILS

Robert of Arbrissel died Friday, February 25, 1116, at the hour
when monks chant the prayer service of the day's end. His body
was not yet near finding rest. Gathered around Robert's mortal remains, the brothers and sisters of Fontevraud decided to conceal
his death. Quickly, they picked up the body not yet washed or
shrouded, carried it out of the little room where he died, a kind of
sacristy near the chapel, took it to the nuns' cloister, and locked it
in. They were counting on the respect due to the abode of God's
brides. Instead, the heat of the chase took over the warriors who
stood guard. Alard forgot the oath extorted from him without a
second thought. These men, Leger's and Geoffrey of Issoudun's,
ran to poach on their enemies' preserve. They broke through the

50. Liturgical candles are often marked to keep time as they burn down.

51. Miserere, meaning "Have mercy," is the name of a prayer that is important
in numerous liturgical services. In this case, Robert specifically asks for the mercy
of Jesus, Mary, angels and archangels, and the saints. The Confiteor ("I confess")
and Pater Noster ("Our Father") are parts of the liturgy of the Mass; saying the latter is often assigned as penance.

doors, seized the body, and placed it, like a trophy, in the chapel where the lords of Berry had established their camp. This little world was cut in two. Each side closeted itself to reckon its forces. The men of Berry had the clear advantage. Faced with a small group of monks and nuns more expert in psalmody than mêlée and isolated in enemy territory, the local party included men at arms and warlords. If the people of Fontevraud had rallied Orsan with every care and if neighboring priories and perhaps even the motherhouse had come to the rescue, their adversaries still had the inexhaustible resources of the nearby countryside.

The matter quickly became public and a crowd of provincials assembled, mourning Robert's death less than they rejoiced at a windfall, "that God had adorned their diocese with such as saintly person who, as they believe, would intercede for them in paradise." Knowing "that they could not otherwise chase away this crowd of laypeople," the brothers and sisters asked to be allowed at least to enshroud the master. This was permitted. On Saturday, they clothed Robert's body in a hairshirt and robe, a hermit's outfit that recalled his preferred life.[52] They put him in a coffin and performed a funeral of sorts amidst sobbing. They began vigils and fasting.

To this point, Petronilla had held her fire, waiting for the right moment. The arrival of nobles from Bourges gave her representatives to her taste, people from her own world. She complained to them of the wrong done her and asked them to intercede on her behalf with their archbishop. Appealed to in this way, Leger mellowed and said he would take up the matter with the people of his province and reply the next day—but his resolve remained strong, for he began to have a stone coffin made for his friend, the better to secure him in the soil of Orsan. A magnificent array of the province's notables assembled, regular and secular clergy, nobles,

52. For the events of Saturday through the following Tuesday discussed in the next several paragraphs, see Andreas, *Second Life*, sections 56–63 (Dalarun, *L'impossible sainteté*, 291–294; Venarde, *Robert of Arbrissel*, 58–61).

and others. The group confirmed Leger's decision. A delegation of lords went to report the decision to Petronilla, explaining that they were keeping "the body of the good father that was given to them by the grace of God. . . . For if God had wanted Robert to be buried at Fontevraud, He would not have allowed him to die in these parts. It should suffice for them that they knew his counsel and intimate companionship more than any others alive and to allow him to them in death, since they had had him so rarely during his lifetime." This last parry was inevitable, the same one the people of Poitou made with those of Tours with regard to keeping the body of St. Martin at Candes. The theological argument seemed still more unanswerable: wasn't this a matter of opposing the dictates of Providence rather than merely wanting to change the course of events?

Petronilla had great strength. She did not argue; she shouted. First, she warned the archbishop's spokesmen that she would appeal to the papal legate and to Rome, in conformity with Robert's instructions. The tone grew shriller. If necessary, she would appeal to God, for "there is no pope, king, prince, or person so powerful that the Judge of fairness will not do justice concerning him." The blow hit home. The people of Berry, who had thought the matter was risk-free, now found themselves face-to-face with a powerful network of influence, with an ecclesiastical hierarchy superior to their archbishop, and especially with totally unexpected resistance from a frightened little band. "Quite taken aback," they reported the results of the meeting to Leger and announced that they were withdrawing from the matter. They were laymen with no jurisdiction in a matter that concerned only the archbishop. They also warned him that he would be accountable for his actions on Judgment Day. Petronilla of Chemillé, in one assault, had broken the apparent harmony of the opposition. Here were laymen more Gregorian than clerics, resolving not to interfere in the spiritual realm. They packed up their camp. Leger was reduced to the forces of his own household. His people whispered in his ear that he should take the body to Bourges without delay, perhaps reckoning on the advantage they might gain from having it. Now in doubt, the archbishop did not reply.

On Monday, the nuns processed around their building barefoot and without cloaks, wearing nothing more on this early winter morning than their robes and veils. Entering the chapel, they swore over the holy corpse that they would neither eat nor drink until they obtained satisfaction. Leger went to them, moved by their excesses. "You know how I gave of myself to you and how I love this place; even how I have chosen to be buried here. I rejoiced greatly that God had given me such a companion as Robert and wanted to keep him here so I could be buried at his feet." Already Leger was speaking of his desire in the past tense. He no longer believed it would be satisfied. Ever since agreeing to a discussion, on Saturday, he had watched his advantage diminish. Now he worried about the sisters' health and begged them to put on their cloaks and eat and drink. Bewildered, he asked for a truce. "Pray Our Lord that it please Him to inspire me about what to do." Petronilla appreciated the old saw about striking while the iron is hot. "Certainly we are no longer your daughters and will not pray for you and yours until you return our good father to us. Know this: if he had wanted to be buried here he would not have instructed us otherwise, nor entreated you to have him carried to Fontevraud and to perform the funeral there yourself!"

Each party's interests had been frankly expressed since the beginning of the clash; two logics had confronted each other. For Leger, the order of things is the one chosen by God, and it was for man to give himself up to it. For Robert and Petronilla, now the agent of his desires, order concerned callings stronger than ordinary law. Fontevraud was the principal piece of a project that had to be fulfilled, against all opposition, even against apparent divine

will that caused the saint to die on foreign soil. Didn't Jacob rob
Esau of his birthright? Didn't he usurp Isaac's benediction? Yet he
was also called Israel, who did not fear to wrestle with God, hand-
to-hand, in a nocturnal embrace and who, by the steps of the mystical ladder, attained the sight of God, face to face.[53] In the course of
every saint's life, there is a time of apparent revolt that actually un-
veils the plan God concealed from men. "And the good archbishop,
hearing this reply, went away very sad," like a certain rich young
man who came to understand where the truth lay.[54]

On Tuesday, Leger summoned the abbess and some of her ad-
visors. He nobly admitted defeat and his confession raised him
above the level of a victor.

"I see clearly that you are still determined in your purpose and will
not be comforted if you do not get what you ask. I tell you: the compassion I have for you constrains me. I bear witness before God that what I
have done was for nothing other than the love I bore for Robert, and I
very much wanted him buried here so I could be placed at his feet. I believe that it would have profited me to be accompanied by such a holy
personage before Our Lord. Therefore, pardon me and mine for what we
have done and the pain we have caused you. Stay again today, and tomorrow you will depart under the protection of Our Lord. And just as your
good master beseeched and requested of me, with God's help I will go
and perform the funeral myself."

Fontevraud won the day. Petronilla had managed an extraordinary
reversal of fortune. Leger of Bourges fell victim, in the end, to his
own sincerity. Fidelity to a friend triumphed over the possessive
passion of friendship. As a consolation prize, Robert's heart was left
to the priory in Berry. Andreas does not say so, nor did he note,
since he wrote too soon, that when the archbishop died in 1120, he

---

53. Gn 25:29–34, 27:1–36, 32:25–31, and 28:10–16 recount these four incidents in the life of Jacob.

54. The incident of Jesus and the rich young man: Mt 19:16–22.

left to the nuns of Orsan the residence he had acquired there. He was buried in the church, his tomb next to a pyramid that contained his friend's heart. On the mausoleum was this epitaph:

He loved Robert so much during his life that he did not want to be separated from his heart after death.[55]

The holy body at last escaped. On Wednesday, a fine array took to the road.[56] Twenty miles to the north was the point of embarkation on the Cher, and from there the watercourse ran to the Loire. As it went along, the funeral procession grew with the addition of prelates and barons until, on the following Sunday, it docked at the port of Candes. From the abbey a mile or so south, the brothers and sisters of Fontevraud went down to meet the coffin, as did the people of the village, "from the least to the greatest." At the confluence of the Loire and the Vienne, the people of Candes waited, too, on solid ground. In 397, their distant ancestors had seen the body of the great St. Martin escape their grasp. It slipped up the river as far as Tours, while on the water spring came again in the middle of autumn for the brief moment called St. Martin's summer.[57] In this early March of 1116, the people of Candes wanted to hold onto Robert, sent from heaven, for one night, they said, and if possible forever. Burned by the Orsan affair, the party of Fontevraud turned a deaf ear. So the people of Candes, armed with swords and cudgels, aimed at "harming, striking, and hurting the religious." The latter,

55. Deshoulières, "Le prieuré d'Orsan," 96–98; between pages 96 and 97 there is a reproduction of seventeenth-century sketch of the pyramidal structure containing Robert's heart and, at its feet, Leger's tomb with its legend, in Latin "Quippe in tantum coluerat Robertus quum vivus esset ut mortuus ab ejus corde noluerit removeri."

56. The story of Robert's final return to Fontevraud and his burial there is recounted in Andreas, *Second Life*, sections 64–68 (Dalarun, *L'impossible sainteté*, 294–296; Venarde, *Robert of Arbrissel*, 61–63).

57. In English, the expression is "Indian summer." St. Martin died in early November, probably in the year 397.

like their master among the thieves, plunged through the fields in prayer. At this spectacle, their adversaries abandoned the fight and all went together, with no hard feelings, up the valley to Font-evraud.

On Sunday and Monday, the body was watched over in the Great Monastery. Then began a procession worthy of this monastic city. Robert was to be shown everywhere, like a relic in its case. On Monday, he rested at the house of Saint Lazarus among the lepers he loved and who lived there among the others, a little apart. There was a service at the Magdalene, too. On Tuesday, the body passed to Saint John's, the men's priory, but did not stay long before being placed on the square in front of the Great Monastery where a crowd of neighboring people pressed to see it. This is how Robert had envisioned it: the unity of the order sealed over his mortal remains and around it, the unanimity of peoples.

It now remained only to bury the dead man in the mud of Fontevraud as he had wished. There is one last struggle to narrate, one as quick as the flash of a blade in the sun and also decisive. The brothers bustled about the coffin, preparing to bury Robert in the place he had designated. "Although he had instructed that he be buried in the cemetery with his good religious brothers and sisters, still a number of archbishops, abbots and monks, nobles and great lords who were present said that he should be put in the main church." Mud, *humus*, signified Robert's humility, *humilitas*. The body, moved away from the place of due honor, would remind everyone of the spirit in which the founder submitted himself to the sisters and submitted the brothers to them alongside him as a penance.

The noble nuns could not bear what, in the absence of the master, was no more than an affront. They did not even have to do battle themselves, since prelates and barons took up the charge for them, ostensibly desiring to render homage to the dead man but doubtless concerned to uphold the rank of women of their blood, of their world. Raoul of Orléans, archbishop of Tours, Bishop Renaud de Martigné of Angers, a number of abbots, Count Fulk of Anjou, Berlai of Montreuil, Gautier of Montsoreau, Robert of Blois, and Gilbert of Loudun—what weight did a few obscure religious brothers carry in such company? At Orsan, they had managed to place the coarse habit of a hermit over Robert's hairshirt. This sign, too, was effaced and the flesh that had brought on Robert's torment appeared for the last time dressed in priestly garb, tamed and inoffensive.[58] The brothers, shoulders slumped and mouths agape, saw their companion buried in great pomp and great honor.

On this Tuesday, March 7, 1116, the strange and mad Fontevraud of Robert of Arbrissel died. The place remained a retreat for the spare daughters of noble families and world-weary great ladies, joined by their priests and servants. On the right-hand side of the great altar in the abbey church the holy confiscated body of Robert marked the two-fold victory of Petronilla of Chemillé.

Leger of Bourges, who came to preside over the burial service as Robert had asked, stayed until the next day. It is hard to imagine him on that Tuesday, taking his place among the mighty, this same archbishop who, since he so wanted to be buried at his friend's feet, must have well understood the plan for humility. On Wednesday, he made a farewell sermon in the brothers' chapter house, among the defeated. What must they have thought?

58. Two charters containing details about the day of Robert's burial are translated in Venarde, *Robert of Arbrissel*, 110–112.

6

THE DISCIPLE HE LOVED

The Life of a saint does not end with his death or even his burial. At this point, in the great hagiographical tradition, there follow the praises of men, imperfect echoes of a choir of angels. Then come in succession the miracles accomplished through the intercession of the dead saint, particularly those blossoming around his tomb, sprouting most densely over the fertile corpse.

Remembrance of a saint is not limited to the writing of his *vita*. Even before that project was begun, a messenger was sent out to allied abbeys, neighboring cathedrals, chapters, and schools. He carried a long roll of parchment. At its head, a short obituary announced the return of the elect to his Father and recounted the dense array of his unforgettable accomplishments and unparalleled virtues. Hearing the news, each community added its tears, verses, and praises. The precious roll returned to its point of origin months later. It was carefully deposited in the library or archives as a testimony to the influence of the dead one. The mortuary roll of Vitalis of Savigny included more than 200 entries in 200 different hands, a gold mine for paleographers and an ornament for his monastic federation.[1] A cult takes shape: the body is exhumed to confirm its miraculous preservation, then placed in a shrine where pilgrims can enjoy it more readily; a special prayer service is

---

1. Léopold Delisle, *Rouleaux des morts du IXe au XVe siècle* (Paris, 1866), 281–344. Paleographers study the history of handwriting.

devised to commemorate the day of the saint's death. Then, as the tide of miracles, far from receding, rises higher, the stories are recorded in a book of miracles that can prolong the Life indefinitely.

Robert of Arbrissel's consignment to oblivion was carefully orchestrated. There was no mortuary roll, and there long remained uncertainty about the year of his death and, even more incredibly, some wavering about the day of departure to his Father and therefore his feast day. The two charters mentioning his funeral were not included in the Grand Cartulaire, the enormous collection of documents concerning Fontevraud.[2] Agnes, a witness to Robert's death, was sent to the priory of Vega de León in northwestern Spain, the most remote of all Fontevraud's houses, where she could reflect at leisure on the pettiness of parochial interest and the grandeur of obedience.[3] The placement of Robert's tomb was quite effective. Granted an honor he did not want, hidden away by the nuns in the most private part of their sanctuary, Robert was sequestered from both the brothers and the masses. Forbidden to his companions, inaccessible to the people, his tomb was the site of no miracles. The rumor of sanctity faded and died away. The stone tomb sealed his oblivion.

In the seventeenth century, abbesses who wanted to bring disobedient brothers to heel tried to revive the memory of the long-ago founder to legitimize their supremacy. They sought an official canonization from the papacy according to a procedure that had not existed in Robert's time. But in the absence of a cult around the tomb, the dossier was exceedingly thin. Worse, this was a delicate operation, for the search for sanctity also revived the roaring of long-ago scandals. A second attempt, in the nineteenth century,

2. Or at least not in the fragment of this collection that survives.

3. That is, Agnes, who was hesitant to obey Robert's final wishes and appears ultimately to have been neutral in the battle between the parties of Fontevraud and Berry, was reassigned as a penance—or a punishment—far from her native land.

was equally unsuccessful.[4] Robert of Arbrissel is, as it were, still pending.

Petronilla of Chemillé had to have a *vita* written, despite what she thought about the matter. It was the least she could do and therefore the only thing she did. She entrusted the task to Baudri of Bourgueil, the poet-prelate, a literary star of the age. She gave him the least information possible, for he was doing a commissioned work that did not go very far into shocking details and sanitized the saint in a flood of holy water. As we have said, however, Robert's charm was such that even Baudri had been touched by its grace. The first Life was quite unkind to the abbess. The author began by reporting, with displeasing emphasis, that Petronilla had known the marriage bed. Baudri vaunted the merits of Hersende and explained that only death had kept her from occupying the office of abbess. He underlined that Robert had welcomed the poor by preference and that if he did not reject women of the nobility, it was only in conformity with the example of Christ, who rejected nobody. Finally, Baudri exalted desert asceticism, preaching, and the crowds of followers as Robert's most ardent concern.

Petronilla was caught in her own trap. Baudri's reputation was such that she could not hide his account under a bushel. Instead of suppressing it, Petronilla's solution was to balance it with another account. The abbess turned to Andreas, the prior of Saint John and Robert's former chaplain, a literate but unknown man who had shown perfect obedience to Petronilla. She calculated all the advantage she might gain from his account. He was a witness to Robert's last months, including her own election; he was present in the last days, including Petronilla's triumph over an agitated Berry. Center-

---

4. On these activities, see J. M. B. Porter, "Fontevrault Looks Back to Her Founder: Reform and the Attempts to Canonize Robert of Arbrissel," in *The Church Retrospective: Depictions and Interpretations*, ed. R. N. Swanson (Woodbridge, 1997), 361–377.

ing the narrative on these final episodes under cover of completing Baudri's work, the years of excess and wandering could be passed over. Robert would appear as the unruffled founder, the sage whose authority all clergy recognized, called from one end of the realm to the other to preach the good news or settle disputes. Kings, great men, and brigands paid tribute to him, and this uncontroversial man would be the one to transmit his splendid heritage to Petronilla. Instead of literary glory she would take liege service. The second Life would be entirely flattering to the abbess.

Andreas was obedient, as his master had taught him to be. Under the control of women, he lived a quiet asceticism of submission that, he believed, would assure his salvation. Three or four years after Robert died he broke his silence; his voice rose once more, clear, sharp, and intolerable. Andreas bore witness with the deference due his superior but not in the spirit of concession. The spirit in which the submission of men to women was conceived, the permanent rights of the brothers, the carnal tenderness of Robert for his daughters, but also his condescension to them and their foundation, his permanent preference for the desert, Petronilla's rages and blunders, the derided plans for Robert's burial—it is all there. No fewer than eight times, the chaplain reports that the master desired to lie forever in the mud of Fontevraud, as if to make more striking the infidelity to Robert's wishes. Leger of Bourges emerges as greater in defeat, and there is the sense that the narrator preferred the stubbornness of his sincere friendship to the caress of a Judas's kiss.

Some eighteenth-century scholars doubted the attribution of the *Second Life* to Andreas on the grounds that he was present in the narrative and would not have referred to himself in the third person. Thus the spirit of critical enquiry sometimes overcomes good sense. In the disconcerting universe of medieval hagiography, everyone stands in for someone else. More than the Sulpicius Severus of a new St. Martin, the prior of Fontevraud saw himself in the image of John the Evangelist, "the disciple that Jesus loved."[5] In light of this connection, a few points emerge from obscurity. Andreas speaks of himself at that same distance the Evangelist handled so artfully. Along with his brothers, Andreas accepted the charge of women who were only pale reflections of the Virgin Mary, whom John, in his own account, agreed to care for. As on the evening of the Last Supper John received from Christ the revelation that someone would betray him, the chaplain received the dying Robert's last confidences—a speech that, as we have noted, Andreas does not report, as if he hoped to make it a weapon by keeping it secret. Finally, to perfect the resemblance, Andreas was commanded to record the Passion of Robert in a new Gospel. Once again, the faces whose features we try to see, the individuals that we hope to glimpse through what Jacques Le Goff calls "cracks in the discourse,"[6] are set hieratically in the tableau of Calvary to which Robert's life unfailingly returns us, as if to the center of the mystery: John supporting Mary, Mary Magdalene on her knees, and Christ in His abandonment by God.

Petronilla was not a woman to accept the unacceptable. Entering Robert's entourage many years earlier, she escaped the power of the males of her family. She chose one of the few paths where her stubbornness and ambition could have free expression. Around 1122, the death of the unyielding prior gave her free rein. She could not write herself and she despaired of finding a slave pen. I believe (but, however likely, it is only a hypothesis) that Petronilla decided to censor Andreas's account. If it was not she who did it, in any case someone did. The beginning of the work, the part that reported the submission of the brothers and the election of Petronilla, was retained, while the more unendurable end was cut off, skillfully

5. Jn 19:26.
6. Jacques Le Goff, "Saint Louis a-t-il existé?" *L'Histoire* 40 (December 1981), 92 (reprinted in Jacques Le Goff, *Un long Moyen Age* [Paris, 2004], 199).

using an ambiguous passage just after Robert's confession to pass for the announcement of his death.[7] This clever sin of omission was carefully recopied. The truncated Latin Life was gathered up by several scholars in the seventeenth century who published it as the medieval manuscripts vanished.

In one corner of the disorderly archives of Fontevraud there lay forgotten a copy of Andreas's original along with a few other embarrassing documents. It stayed there nearly four hundred years. At the beginning of the sixteenth century, Abbess Renée of Bourbon wanted to discipline the nuns of Fontevraud, at that time living in luxury and suspect freedom. Someone told her about this old manuscript that exalted Robert's destitution and brought noblewomen down a peg or two. Renée gave an obscure brother named Boudet the job of translating this Latin scrawl that was beginning not to be understood very well.[8] Wisely and conscientiously, Boudet set himself to the task, producing the translation of a diligent and at times a bit obtuse Latin student in the pretty language of the sixteenth century, in which the miracle of Menat and the end of Andreas's account are preserved.

In the seventeenth century, the abbesses found themselves at odds not with the nuns but the brothers. The shortened version that had been circulating since the Middle Ages suited their needs perfectly. This little manuscript volume containing the full French version, which no longer interested anybody, came into the hands of a bibliophile, a hard-working scholar. At his death, he left his books to Jean-Baptist Colbert (1619–1683), chief finance minister to King Louis XIV, who also had a notable private library. Boudet's

7. Andreas, *Second Life*, section 42 (PL 162: 1078; Venarde, *Robert of Arbrissel*, 50): "Certum quidem est quod Deus servum suum in hac oratione exaudierit, quem non longe post a vinculis carneis absolutum, a mundi hujus exsilio abstraxit" ("It is certain that God heeded His servant in prayer, since not long afterwards He loosed Robert from the bonds of flesh and removed him from this world's exile").

8. Dalarun, *L'impossible sainteté*, 94–97.

little book thus entered into the collection of this state official but was lost among the volumes amidst which it was included and considered among the least valuable. In the eighteenth century, the Royal Library bought what had been Colbert's collection. Surviving undisturbed across many changes of rule, the volume slept in Paris on the shelves of what become the Bibliothèque Nationale, the French national library, a unique witness to the death of Robert of Arbrissel and the faithfulness of the disciple he loved. It is very small, smaller than a hand, as if to emphasize the fragility of memory.[9]

The long ago story that the present little book retells, in which women triumph over men in the heyday of feudal society, should not lead us to take the exception for the rule. The prior's narrative, recording the double victory of Petronilla of Chemillé, tells also, in a way, of her defeat. Neither of the hagiographers she approached would play her game. If it is the case that she censored Andreas's account, such an ill-tempered and inept move was another powerful indicator of weakness. Never in this affair, as is nearly always the case in the Middle Ages, is the voice of women heard. Even the most powerful still had to pass the pen to clerics to celebrate their triumph and learn, to their expense, that this procedure was not without risk.

Hersende, Petronilla, Angarde, and Agnes, to say nothing of the humbler women who have slipped away forever—who can say exactly what caused them to leave castle, brothel, or husband to follow Robert? Who can tell about the affection he had for them, the strength of their faith? These matters are left to the imagination on almost all counts. The texts are against them: when they

---

9. Dalarun, *L'impossible sainteté*, 108–114, describes the history of this tiny manuscript (about 3½ x 5 inches) since the sixteenth century. It was Dalarun who discovered it in the Bibliothèque Nationale in Paris.

refuse to play timid virgins or repentant sinners, we are forced to recall them as viragos.

At Rouen and Menat, with a faint tremor of the fractured soul that neared the end of its long and winding road, Robert of Arbrissel for an instant shook the very thick, ancient, and durable walls built between men and women, between those who have words and power and those reduced to silence, while his mutilated Life is a backhand testimony to the omnipotence of the word and those who control it.

TRANSLATOR'S NOTE
AND ACKNOWLEDGMENTS

For this version of *Robert d'Arbrissel, fondateur de Fontevraud*, I added notes and a full bibliography that were not part of the original 1986 French edition, plus an introduction placing it in the context of other scholarship on Robert of Arbrissel. I have also taken the liberty of leveling out somewhat a prose style that, although charming in French, might seem florid to English speakers if reproduced too literally.

It is a pleasure to thank Jacques Dalarun, who answered numerous questions and meticulously reviewed the entire translation, all with good cheer, enthusiasm, and remarkable efficiency. I am grateful to Jack Eckert, W. Scott Jessee, David McGonagle, and Lara Putnam for help and advice of various kinds. For errors and infelicities in translation, plus any mistakes of fact or judgment in the introduction, notes, or bibliography, the translator is solely responsible.

BIBLIOGRAPHY

NB. Medieval source materials that figure significantly in this book are cited individually in Section I; they are in Latin unless otherwise noted. For collections of sources, see Section II, where they are ordered by the name of modern translator or editor rather than author. All of the texts in Section I.A except the letters of Ivo of Chartres are translated into English in Bruce L. Venarde, *Robert of Arbrissel: A Medieval Religious Life* (Washington, DC, 2003). In Section I.B, the anonymous Lives of saints are in alphabetical order by saints' names.

I. MEDIEVAL DOCUMENTS

A. Materials concerning Robert of Arbrissel

Andreas of Fontevraud. *Vita Altera B. Roberti de Arbrissello* [*Second Life of Robert of Arbrissel*]. *Patrologia cursus completus, Series Latina*, edited by J.-P. Migne, 221 volumes (Paris, 1844–1864; hereafter PL), 162: 1057–1078 (partial Latin text). Also in Jacques Dalarun, *L'impossible sainteté: La Vie retrouvée de Robert d'Arbrissel (v. 1045–1116), fondateur de Fontevraud* (Paris, 1985), 264–299 (late medieval French version).

Baudri of Bourgueil. *Vita Prima B. Roberti de Arbrissello* [*First Life of Robert of Arbrissel*]. PL 162: 1043–1058.

Geoffrey of Vendôme. Letter to Robert of Arbrissel. In *Œuvres* (Paris, 1996), 148–151 (Letter 79; with French translation), edited by Geneviève Giordanengo, and in PL 157: 181–184 (Book 4, Letter 47).

Hildebert of Lavardin (?). Epitaph for Robert of Arbrissel. PL 171: 1391–1392.

Ivo of Chartres. Letters 34 and 37. In Yves de Chartres, *Correspondance*, volume 1, edited by Jean Leclercq (Paris, 1949), 138–141 and 152–157 (with French translation), and in PL 162: 46, 49–50.

Marbode of Rennes. Letter to Robert of Arbrissel. In Johannes van Walter, *Die ersten Wanderprediger Frankreichs. Studien zur Geschichte des Mönchtums,* 2 volumes (Leipzig, 1903–1906), 1: 181–189; and partial version in PL 171: 1480–1486 (as Letter 6).

Robert of Arbrissel. Letter to Ermengarde. In "Lettre inédite de Robert d'Arbrissel à la comtesse Ermengarde," edited by Jules de Pétigny. *Bibliothèque de l'Ecole des Chartes* 15 (1854): 225–235 (with French translation).

B. Other medieval texts cited

Anonymous. "Life of St. Alexis." Translated by Nancy Vine Durling in Thomas F. Head, ed. *Medieval Hagiography: An Anthology* (New York, 2000), 317–340 (English translation only).

Anonymous. *Vita prima sancti Carilefi [First Life of Calais]*. Edited by Laurentius Surius in *De probatis sanctorum historiis,* 7 volumes (Cologne, 1576–1586), 7: 32–39.

Anonymous. *Vita Carileffi [Life of Calais]*. Edited by B. Krusch in *Monumenta Germaniae Historica, Scriptorum Rerum Merovingicarum* (Hannover, 1885–), 3: 386–394.

Anonymous. *Vita Carilefi [Life of Calais]*. *Acta sanctorum quotquot toto orbe coluntur,* 68 volumes (Antwerp, 1634–1940; reprinted Brussels, 1965–1970; hereafter AASS), July, volume 1, 90–99.

Anonymous. *Vita B. Giraldi de Salis [Life of the Blessed Gerald of Sales]*. AASS, October, volume 10, 254–267.

Anonymous. *Vita Menelei [Life of Meneleus]*. AASS, July, volume 5, 308–319.

[Anonymous.] *Vie de Saint Etienne d'Obazine [Life of Saint Stephen of Obazine]*. Edited and translated by Michel Aubrun (Clermont-Ferrand, 1970; Latin text and French translation).

Anonymous. *Life of Thaïs*. Translated in Benedicta Ward, *Harlots of the Desert: A Study of Repentance in Early Monastic Sources* (Kalamazoo, MI, 1987), 83–84 (English translation only).

Anonymous. *Vita S. Theofredi [Life of Saint Theofrid]*. AASS, October, volume 8, 527–533.

Athanasius. "The Life of Anthony." Translated by Carolinne White in *Early Christian Lives* (New York, 1998), 1–70 (English translation only).

Benedict of Nursia. *Rule*. Latin text and translation into several languages at www.osb.org/rb.

Bernard of Clairvaux. Letter to Ermengarde. PL 182: 262–263 and translated by Bruno Scott James in *The Letters of Saint Bernard of Clairvaux* (Kalamazoo, MI, 1998), 181–182.

Etienne de Fougères. *Vita B. Vitalis [Life of the Blessed Vitalis]*. Edited by E.-P. Sauvage in *Analecta Bollandiana* 1 (1882), 355–390.

Etienne de Fougères (?). *Vita S. Firmati [Life of Saint Firmatus]*. Edited by E.-A. Pigeon in *Vies des saints du diocèse de Coutances et Avranches*, 2 volumes (Avranches, 1892–1898), 2: 378–417 (Latin text with French translation), and in AASS, April, volume 3, 334–341 (Latin only).

Geoffrey the Fat. *Vita S. Bernardi [Life of Saint Bernard of Tiron]*. In Bernard Beck, *Saint Bernard de Tiron: l'ermite, le moine et le monde* (Cormelles-le-Royal, 1998), 312–461 (Latin text with French translation) and in PL 172: 1367–1446.

Geoffrey of Vendôme. Letter to Pope Pascal. Edited by Geneviève Giordanengo in *Œuvres* (Paris, 1996), 272–281 (Letter 134; Latin text with French translation), and in PL 157: 42–46 (Book 1, Letter 7).

———. Letter to Hamelinus. Edited by Geneviève Giordanengo in *Œuvres* (Paris, 1996), 2–5 (Letter 1; Latin text with French translation), and in PL 157: 167–168 (Book 4, Letter 24).

———. Letter to Ermengarde. Edited by Geneviève Giordanengo in *Œuvres* (Paris, 1996), 142–143 (Letter 75; Latin text with French translation), and in PL 157: 205 (Book 5, Letter 23).

Gregory of Tours. *History of the Franks*. Translated by Lewis Thorpe. Harmondsworth, 1974 (English translation only).

Jerome. "Life of Paul of Thebes." Translated by Carolinne White in *Early Christian Lives* (New York, 1998), 71–84 (English translation only).

John Cassian. *The Conferences*. Translated by Boniface Ramsey. New York, 1997 (English translation only).

Marbode of Rennes. Poem to Ermengarde ("M. episcopus E. comitissae"). PL 171: 1659–1660.

Peter the Venerable. Letter to His Brothers (Letter 53). In *The Letters of Peter the Venerable*, edited by Giles Constable, 2 volumes (Cambridge, MA, 1967), 1: 153–173.

Peter Damian. *Vita beati Romualdi [Life of the Blessed Romuald]*. Edited by Giovanni Tabacco (Rome, 1957) and in PL 144: 953–1008. Partial English translation by Henrietta Leyser in Thomas F. Head, ed., *Medieval Hagiography: An Anthology* (New York, 2000), 295–316.

Pseudo-Dionysius: The Complete Works. Translated by Colm Luibhéid et al. New York, 1987 (English translation only).

Suger. *The Deeds of Louis the Fat*. Translated by Richard Cusimano and John Moorhead. Washington, DC, 1992 (English translation only).

Sulpicius Severus. Letter to Bassula. PL 20: 180–184.

———. "Life of Martin of Tours." Translated by Carolinne White, *Early Christian Lives*, 129–159 (English translation only).

William of Malmesbury. *Gesta Regum Anglorum: The History of the English Kings*. Edited by R. A. B. Mynors et al., 2 volumes. Oxford, 1998–1999 (Latin text and English translation).

II. MEDIEVAL SOURCE COLLECTIONS
AND MODERN STUDIES

Acta sanctorum quotquot toto orbe coluntur, 68 volumes. Antwerp, 1634 (reprinted Brussels, 1965–1970).

Barthélemy, Dominique. "Le renoncement aux ordalies." In *Robert d'Arbrissel et la vie religieuse dans l'Ouest de la France*, edited by Jacques Dalarun, 173–197. Turnhout, 2004.

Bartlett, Robert. *Trial by Fire and Water: The Medieval Judicial Ordeal*. New York, 1986.

Beck, Bernard. *Saint Bernard de Tiron: l'ermite, le moine et le monde*. Cormelles-le-Royal, 1998.

Beech, George T. "Biography and the Study of 11th Century Society: Bishop Peter II of Poitiers (1087–1115)." *Francia* 7 (1979): 101–121.

Bezzola, Reto R. *Les origines et la formation de la littérature courtoise en Occident (500–1200)*, 3 volumes. Paris, 1944–1963.

Bienvenu, Jean-Marc. *L'étonnant fondateur de Fontevraud: Robert d'Arbrissel*. Paris, 1981.

Bienvenu, Jean-Marc, et al. *Grand Cartulaire de Fontevraud*. Poitiers, 2000– .

Blamires, Alcuin. *Woman Defamed and Woman Defended: An Anthology of Medieval Texts*. Oxford, 1992.

Bloch, Marc. *The Historian's Craft*. Translated by Peter Putnam. New York, 1953 [French original 1949].

Bond, Gerald. *The Poetry of William VII, Count of Poitiers, IX Duke of Aquitaine*. New York, 1982.

Caby, Cécile. "Vies parallèles: ermites d'Italie et de la France de l'Ouest (Xᵉ–XIIᵉ siècle)." In *Robert d'Arbrissel et la vie religieuse dans l'Ouest de la France*, edited by Jacques Dalarun, 11–24. Turnhout, 2004.

Certeau, Michel de. *The Writing of History*. Translated by Tom Conley. New York, 1988 [French original 1975].

Cizek, Alexandru. "Le saint comme martyr et psychagogue: quelques remarques sur l'image ambiguë de Robert d'Arbrissel dans les sources littéraires latines." *Hagiographica* 9 (2002): 45–72.

Constable, Giles. *The Letters of Peter the Venerable*, 2 volumes. Cambridge, MA, 1967.

Cowdrey, H. E. J. *Pope Gregory VII, 1073–1085.* Oxford, 1998.

Dalarun, Jacques. "Fortune institutionnelle, littéraire, et historiographique de Robert d'Arbrissel." In *Robert d'Arbrissel et la vie religieuse dans l'Ouest de la France*, edited by Jacques Dalarun, 293–322. Turnhout, 2004.

———. *L'impossible sainteté: La Vie retrouvée de Robert d'Arbrissel (v.1045–1116), fondateur de Fontevraud.* Paris, 1985.

———. *Robert d'Arbrissel et la vie religieuse dans l'Ouest de la France.* Turnhout, 2004.

Delisle, Léopold. *Rouleaux des morts du IXe au XVe siècle.* Paris, 1866.

Deshoulières, F. "Le prieuré d'Orsan en Berri." *Mémoires de la société des antiquaires du Centre* 25 (1901): 51–137.

Duby, Georges. *The Knight, the Lady, and the Priest: The Making of Modern Marriage in Medieval France.* Translated by Barbara Bray. New York, 1983 [French original 1981].

———. *William Marshall: The Flower of Chivalry.* Translated by Richard Howard. New York, 1985 [French original 1984].

Frugoni, Arsenio. *Arnaldo da Brescia nelle fonti del secolo XII.* Rome, 1954.

Giordanengo, Geneviève. [*Geoffroy de Vendôme:*] *Œuvres.* Paris, 1996.

Gold, Penny Schine. *The Lady and the Virgin: Image, Attitude, and Experience in Twelfth-Century France.* Chicago, 1985.

Golding, Brian. *Gilbert of Sempringham and the Gilbertine Order, c. 1130–c. 1300.* Oxford, 1995.

Green, Karen. "What Becomes a Legend Most: Robert of Arbrissel and His Prostitute Following." M.A. thesis, Columbia University, 1994.

Head, Thomas F. *Medieval Hagiography: An Anthology.* New York, 2000.

Iogna-Prat, Dominique. "La femme dans la perspective pénitentielle des ermites du Bas-Maine (fin XIe–début XIIe siècle)." *Revue d'histoire de la spiritualité* 53 (1977): 47–64.

James, Bruno Scott. *The Letters of Saint Bernard of Clairvaux.* Kalamazoo, MI, 1998.

Jessee, W. Scott. "Robert d'Arbrissel: Aristocratic Patronage and the Question of Heresy." *Journal of Medieval History* 20 (1994): 221–235.

Karras, Ruth Mazo. *Common Women: Prostitution and Sexuality in Medieval England.* New York, 1996.

Kerr, Berenice M. *Religious Life for Women, c. 1100–c. 1350: Fontevraud in England.* Oxford, 1999.

Lacarrière, Jacques. *Les hommes ivres de Dieu.* Paris, 1975.

Le Goff, Jacques. "Saint Louis a-t-il existé?" *L'Histoire* 40 (December 1981): 90–99. Reprinted in *Un long Moyen Age* (Paris, 2004), 195–215.

———. *Time, Work and Culture in the Middle Ages.* Translated by Arthur Goldhammer. Chicago, 1980 [French original 1977].

Leclercq, Jean [*Yves de Chartres:*] *Correspondance.* Volume 1. Paris, 1949.

Lurio, Melissa Belleville. "An Educated Bishop in an Age of Reform: Marbode, Bishop of Rennes, 1096–1123." Ph.D. thesis, Boston University, 2003.

Lynch, Joseph H. *Simoniacal Entry into Religious Life from 1000 to 1260.* Columbus, OH, 1976.

Magistri, Yves. *Baston de deffence et mirouer des professeurs de la vie reguliere de l'Abbaye de l'Ordre de Fontevraud.* Angers, 1586.

Michelet, Jules. *Œuvres complètes,* 21 volumes. Paris, 1971–1982.

Migne, J.-P. *Patrologia cursus completus, Series latina,* 221 volumes. Paris, 1844–1864.

Moolenbroek, Jaap van. *Vital l'ermite, prédicateur itinérant, fondateur de l'abbaye normande de Savigny.* Translated by Anne-Marie Nambot. Assen, 1990.

Moore, R. I. *The First European Revolution, ca. 970–1215.* Oxford, 2000.

———. *The Origins of European Dissent.* New York, 1977.

Morris, Colin. *The Papal Monarchy: The Western Church from 1050 to 1250.* Oxford, 1989.

Nabokov, Vladimir. *The Real Life of Sebastian Knight.* Norwalk, CT, 1941.

Patrologia cursus completes. See Migne.

Pernoud, Régine. *Women in the Days of the Cathedrals.* Translated and adapted by Anne Côté-Harriss. San Francisco, 1998 [French original 1980].

Pétigny, Jules de. "Lettre inédite de Robert d'Arbrissel à la comtesse Ermengarde." *Bibliothèque de l'Ecole des Chartes* 15 (1854): 209–235.

———. "Robert d'Arbrissel et Geoffroi de Vendôme." *Bibliothèque de l'Ecole des Chartes* 15 (1854): 1–30.

Picavet, François. *Roscelin: Philosophe et théologien.* Paris, 1911.

Pichot, Daniel. "Robert d'Arbrissel, le solitaire et la multitude." *Oribus* 53 (2001): 51–62.

Porter, J. M. B. "Fontevrault Looks Back to Her Founder: Reform and the Attempts to Canonize Robert of Arbrissel." In *The Church Ret-*

rospective: Depictions and Interpretations, edited by R. N. Swanson, 361–377. Woodbridge, 1997.

Prigent, Daniel. "Le cadre de vie à Fontevraud dans la seconde moitié du XIIᵉ siècle." *Fontevraud: Histoire-Archéologie* 5 (1997–1998): 39–56.

————. "Fontevraud au début du XIIᵉ siècle: Les premiers temps d'une communauté monastique." In *Robert d'Arbrissel et la vie religieuse dans l'Ouest de la France*, edited by Jacques Dalarun, 255–279. Turnhout, 2004.

Rossiaud, Jacques. *Medieval Prostitution.* Translated by Lydia G. Cochrane. New York, 1988 [Italian original 1984].

Ryan, John. *Irish Monasticism: Origins and Early Development.* London, 1931.

Simmons, Loraine. "The Abbey Church at Fontevraud in the Later Twelfth Century: Anxiety, Authority and Architecture in the Female Spiritual Life." *Gesta* 31 (1992): 99–107.

Smith, Jacqueline. "Robert of Arbrissel: *Procurator mulierum.*" In *Medieval Women*, edited by Derek Baker, 175–184. Oxford, 1978.

Souchet, Jean-Baptiste. *Histoire du diocèse et de la ville de Chartres*, 4 volumes. Chartres, 1866–1873.

Touati, François-Olivier. "Saint-Lazare, Fontevraud, Jérusalem." In *Robert d'Arbrissel et la vie religieuse dans l'Ouest de la France*, edited by Jacques Dalarun, 199–237. Turnhout, 2004.

Toubert, Pierre. "Hérésies et réforme ecclésiastique en Italie au XIᵉ et au XIIᵉ siècles. A propos de deux études récentes." *Revue des études italiennes*, n.s. 8 (1961), 58–71.

Van Engen, John. "The Christian Middle Ages as an Historiographical Problem." *American Historical Review* 91 (1986): 519–552.

Vauchez, André. *Sainthood in the Later Middle Ages.* Translated by Jean Birrell. New York, 1997 [French original 1981].

————. *The Spirituality of the Medieval West: From the Eighth to the Twelfth Century.* Translated by Colette Friedlander. Kalamazoo, MI, 1993 [French original 1975].

Venarde, Bruce L. *Robert of Arbrissel: A Medieval Religious Life.* Washington, DC, 2003.

————. *Women's Monasticism and Medieval Society: Nunneries in France and England, 890–1215.* Ithaca, NY, 1997.

Ward, Benedicta. *The Desert Fathers: Sayings of the Early Christian Monks.* London, 2003.

————. *Harlots of the Desert: A Study of Repentance in Early Monastic Sources.* Kalamazoo, MI, 1987.

Walter, Johannes von. *Die ersten Wanderprediger Frankreichs. Studien zur Geschichte des Mönchtums*, 2 volumes. Leipzig, 1903–1906.

Werner, Ernst. *Pauperes Christi: Studien zu sozial-religiösen Bewegungen im Zeitalter des Reformpapsttums*. Leipzig, 1956.

White, Carolinne. *Early Christian Lives*. New York, 1998.

INDEX

Robert of Arbrissel was designed and composed in
Bell by Kachergis Book Design of Pittsboro, North Carolina.
It was printed on 60-pound Natural Offset and bound by
McNaughton & Gunn of Saline, Michigan.